"Moms, grandmothers, teachers, and friends—don't miss the opportunity to give this book to the special young woman you love. The principles contained in it will change their lives forever."

TERRY MEEUWSEN,
COHOST OF *THE 700 CLUB*

"Lisa Ryan lives her life with a passion for God that is evidenced by the rivers of love and concern that flow forth from her toward others. Beautiful on the outside, her inner beauty far surpasses that which can be seen. This book is Lisa's heart on paper, a true challenge for all women to rise up and seize the moment, be risk takers, and allow God to work through us as 'modern-day Esthers.' You will be challenged and inspired by this woman to break out of your containment and become a history maker for the kingdom. Go for it!"

NANCY ALCORN,
MERCY MINISTRIES OF AMERICA

"Yeah! I am so excited about this book and the impact that it will have on so many lives. This book is for the young girl who dreams of doing and being something great for God, the teenager with questions and mistakes, and the woman who still believes that God can make the ordinary extraordinary. Great job, Lisa! You deserve a standing O."

NICOLE C. MULLEN,
DOVE AWARD–WINNING SINGER/SONGWRITER,
"ON MY KNEES" AND "REDEEMER"

forsuchatimeasthis

YOUR IDENTITY,
PURPOSE,
AND PASSION

lisa ryan

Multnomah® Publishers *Sisters, Oregon*

FOR SUCH A TIME AS THIS
published by Multnomah Publishers, Inc.
© 2001 by Lisa Ryan

International Standard Book Number: 1-57673-785-3

Cover image by Digital Vision
Background cover image by Artville

Scripture quotations are from:
The Holy Bible, New International Version © 1973, 1984 by International Bible Society,
used by permission of Zondervan Publishing House
New American Standard Bible (NASB) © 1960, 1977 by the Lockman Foundation
The Holy Bible, New King James Version (NKJV)
© 1984 by Thomas Nelson, Inc.
The Holy Bible, King James Version (KJV)
Holy Bible, New Living Translation (NLT)
© 1996. Used by permission of Tyndale House Publishers, Inc.
All rights reserved.
New Revised Standard Version (NRSV) © 1989 by the Division of Christian Education of the National
Council of the Churches of Christ in the United States of America
The Message © 1993 by Eugene H. Peterson
The Living Bible (TLB) © 1971. Used by permission of Tyndale House Publishers, Inc.

All rights reserved.

Multnomah is a trademark of Multnomah Publishers, Inc.,
and is registered in the U.S. Patent and Trademark Office.
The colophon is a trademark of Multnomah Publishers, Inc.
Printed in the United States of America

For information:
MULTNOMAH PUBLISHERS, INC. • POST OFFICE BOX 1720 • SISTERS, OREGON 97759

Library of Congress Cataloging-in-Publication Data:
Ryan, Lisa. For such a time as this / by Lisa Ryan.   p. cm. ISBN 1-57673-785-3 (pbk.)
1. Bible. O.T. Esther—Criticism, interpretation, etc. 2. Esther, Queen of Persia. I. Title.
BS1375.2 .R93 2001 222'.906—dc21
2001002175

05 06 07—10 9 8 7

dedication

...forsuchatimeasthis

To My Daughters:

Quinlyn Esther Hope
Logan Alister Grace
Madelin Elise Faith

My young Esthers in training.

TABLE OF CONTENTS

foreword

From the moment I met Lisa Ryan, I knew that we were kindred spirits. And after hearing about her vision for this book, I knew that we would forever be sisters of the heart. I spend a large portion of my life hanging out with teenage and college age girls—my "little sistas." I can't count how many times they've heard me read, paraphrase, or try to act out the story of Esther. It's one of my all-time favorites! So when Lisa said that she was writing a book about how to be a modern-day Esther, I was thrilled.

Maybe Esther's story is where Cinderella's story got its start. In the book of Esther an orphaned teenage girl goes from obscurity to stardom. She is beautiful, obedient, and courageous. She also has a secret that could cost her her life. Who she is and what she does in the face of crisis is a model of godliness for all women, but especially for my little sisters everywhere who wonder if God can do something special in their lives.

The God of the past is the same God today, and He'll be the same God tomorrow. Whether you live in the projects, the suburbs, or a palace, God wants to turn the mundane into the magnificent—an ordinary girl into someone extraordinary. Who knows, you might be the one He uses to deliver your family, your community, or your nation. Why not? Because you're a girl? He's done it before and He can do it again…for such a time as this.

Nicole C. Mullen

...forsuchatimeasthis

My deepest heartfelt gratitude to:

God, for making the lessons of Esther real in my life and for the inspiration and faithfulness to bring this message. I'm just a scribe.

Marcus Ryan, my husband and in-house editor, for believing in me more than I ever believed in myself. You always knew this day would come. Thanks so much for being superdad and running interference all those months so I could write. I love you as well for your patience to "talk it through" when I was blocked. I am the woman I am because you love me.

"Seven choice maidens" for supporting me in prayer: Darlene Sala (the Proverbs 31 woman), Karen Conkle, Kim Newton, Diane Chandler, Janet White, Kristy Stekle (my right-hand maiden of research), and Sharon Jehlen (my partner in editing and ideas).

Harold Sala and Gordon Robertson for supporting my research habit with Bible software computer programs. Thanks for investing in me. I'll become a woman of the Word yet.

Dad, for your faithful Sunday night phone calls. I love you.

Mom, for your extended trips to Virginia and helping on the home front so I could write. You've always been there for me.

My CBN sisters and a multitude of friends and family, who helped pray this thing through.

Multnomah Publishers, for believing in this project, and all who made it a reality: Don Jacobson, Bill Jensen, Larry Libby, Judith St. Pierre, Jennifer Gott, Steffany Woolsey, Steve Gardner, and countless others whose eyes, hands, and hearts have touched this project. I never knew how many people it took to publish a book!

chapter one

It's a Girl Thing

...forsuchatimeasthis

This girl, who was also known as Esther.

ESTHER 2:7

With all the things you could be doing and with all the information at your fingertips, why should you read a book about some dead queen named Esther? Is she any relation to your great-aunt Esther, who still pinches your cheek and comments on "how big you're getting" every time you see her?

There's plenty of material out there telling us who we are and how we should behave as women, girls—females. There are volumes of magazine articles giving "girlfriend" advice on everything from bangles and boyfriends to sex appeal and spiritual journeys. But if you've picked up this book and read this far, it's because you're looking for more than just a girl thing. You're also looking for a God thing. In my own desire to understand the true power and beauty of a woman who is

WARNING:

If you're a guy and you've mistakenly picked up this book, I have it on good authority that you won't "get it." I'm telling you right now that this is a chick book. Give it to your girlfriend or sister. She'll love you for it.

fully surrendered to God, I've often been drawn to the story of Esther.

So, ladies, if you're ready to explore what girl power really means, let's take a look at this Old Testament teenager that calls out the Esther in all of us, *for such a time as this*.

Years ago during my reign as Miss California (you notice that I'm not giving the year ☺), I was intrigued to discover that God had included a pageant—of sorts—in the Bible. Who would ever think that smack-dab in the middle of the Old Testament, sandwiched between a couple of guys named Nehemiah and Job, God would include a chick book about a woman named Esther? Who was this girl, and what did she do to get her own book in the Bible? Her Jewish name was Hadassah, but the Persian name she was given, Esther, means *star*. How appropriate since, as we will see, she is the star of the show.

Think of it. The Bible is filled with stories about great men of God that teach us many lessons. Decades of Sunday school lessons have focused on great men of faith: Noah, Abraham, Joseph, Moses, David, John the Baptist, and Paul, to name just a few. Each of these figures was used at some point as God's "man of the hour" to accomplish something significant in history. Each was groomed, equipped, and called by God for a specific time and purpose. But when it came to touching the heart of a king in order to save God's people from annihilation, what did God need? Whom did He choose for this dangerous assignment?

A girl. That's right, a female—a genuine XX-chromosome creation.

There are times when the situation calls for a more delicate approach, something a bit more subtle and disarming. There are times when a guy just doesn't have what it takes. There are times when a girl can influence the world in ways that a guy can't. That's when a girl thing becomes a God thing.

> If you haven't read the book of Esther, put *this* book down and read her story right away. Even if you are familiar with it, read it again so we're all on the same page. I'll wait…. ☺

Okay. You with me? Let's review the cast of characters for future reference since we'll be referring to them throughout the book.

ESTHER	*the star (the queen, formerly known as Hadassah)*
VASHTI	*Esther's predecessor, who is dethroned*
MORDECAI	*Esther's older cousin, who is also her adoptive father*
HEGAI	*supervisor of the "pageant"*
KING XERXES	*king of Persia (also called Ahaseurus in some versions)*
HAMAN	*senior dude next to the king, full of pride and hatred, a major racist*

As we explore this story of divine destiny, we'll find out that Esther possessed a lot of character traits that allowed her to be used by God. But the very first thing we learn about her is that she's a girl, with all the unique characteristics that make a girl a girl.

WE'RE DIFFERENT

Forget everything you've heard about the differences between the sexes being a result of our environment. It's not simply a question of nurture versus nature. Men and women, boys and girls, are different. Those differences are good. The only time in the Creation account when God says something is not good is when He says, "It is not good for the man to be alone" (Genesis 2:18). So what did He do? He created a woman to make His creation complete—and good.

Over the years, Darlene Sala has been a beautiful example to me of a godly woman that is fully at ease with her femininity. Her example has helped me embrace my own role as a Christian woman. In *Created for a Purpose,* Darlene writes about the making of a woman. She points out that God made both Adam and Eve in His image: "So God created man in his own image...male and female he created them" (Genesis 1:27). I really love what she says about the *refinement* of a woman:

> You are a woman descended from Eve, who was created from Adam's rib by the hand of God—and therefore doubly refined at creation.... After God made Adam from the dust of the ground, He took one of Adam's ribs and according to the literal rendering of the Hebrew text, "built He a woman." This double refinement resulted in the remarkable differences between men and women. [1]

Gives a whole new meaning to being a refined lady, doesn't it?

And just look how the New American Standard translates this passage: "The LORD God *fashioned* into a woman the rib which He had taken from the man" (Genesis 2:22, emphasis mine). How appropriate. The first female was *fashioned* from the beginning, and we've been fashioned ever since. That'll shop.

Darlene continues by pointing out that scientists have discovered fairly radical differences in the brain development of prenatal males and females.

> The left side of the brain of a little girl develops more quickly than that of her brother. This results in an ability to better

express herself verbally than her male counterpart.... This produces intuitive reasoning and sensitivity, something men don't have in the same way. Unborn female babies recognize their mothers' voices sooner than do male babies, and after they are born, they can identify faces sooner than their brothers can. [2]

Here's more brain food for you. According to a Web site called BrainPlace.com, women can transfer data between the right and left hemispheres faster than men can. That's why women are multitaskers when it comes to communication. We listen and communicate by using both the logical (left) and creative (right) sides of the brain. Have you ever noticed that women can perform a task while carrying on one conversation and listening to another, taking in not only the facts but also every nuance of voice inflection, body language, mood, and setting?

Part of that has to do with the fact that females have a larger limbic system (the part of the brain that processes our emotions), which is why women are more in touch with their feelings and have a greater need to communicate them. Because of this, women have an increased ability to bond and connect emotionally to others.

You see, by God's design we are relational, intuitive, observant, sensitive, emotional, tenderhearted, compassionate, nurturing creatures. It's the way we're wired. This knowledge gives us the liberty to be the women He created us to be. Since both men and women are made in His image, our uniqueness as females is a direct reflection of the heart of God. And God uses the elements of tenderness, compassion, endurance, self-sacrifice, and the mothering instinct to touch the world in distinctly feminine ways.

GIRL POWER!

Who but a woman like Mother Teresa could have touched the hearts and lives of the suffering and outcast in India with such humility and compassion? In *Heroes,* Dr. Harold Sala (Darlene's husband) writes that at the time of Mother Teresa's death, more than four thousand sisters had joined her in ministering in orphanages, AIDS hospices, and centers for the poor and destitute.

Read Amy Carmichael's story in Elisabeth Elliot's book A Chance to Die (Revell, 1987). While you're at it, read Elisabeth Elliot's story in These Strange Ashes (Vine Books, 1998).

Who but a woman like Amy Carmichael would resolve to work her way through a crowd of angry people in order to rescue a young girl from temple prostitution and then cry with the girl over the pain she had endured? Amy Carmichael, considered a saint by many, is buried under a tree with a gravestone that reads *Ammai,* the Indian word for *mother.*

Who but a woman like Mary Slessor, known as the Queen of Calabar, would fight so passionately for the rights of women and children in Africa? Out of compassion, tenderness, and the loving heart of God, she adopted dozens of babies that had been left to die in the bush. Although born in Scotland, when Mary died in 1915, thousands of Africans wept for *Eka Kpukpro Owo*—"mother of all peoples."

Many books have been written about Mary Slessor. Unfortunately, most of them are out of print. But you can read her story in Mary Slessor: Heroine of Calabar by Basil Miller.

And who but a woman could give birth to the Son of God? Of course, God could have come into this world any old way He wanted. After all, He's God. If He had wanted to come as a grown man, He could have created Jesus the same way He created Adam, with a little dirt, a little spit, and a little puff of breath into his nostrils. But incredibly,

God chose to use a young woman. He chose, by the Holy Spirit, to place His presence in the womb of a virgin girl, who had been specially created to be the bearer of life. No man could have been the vessel to carry Emmanuel—"God with us."

It is often said that the hand that rocks the cradle rules the world. It is possible that the mother in you will nurture, train, and pray for a child who will one day impact the world. You may or may not be there yet, but your role as a mother will affect and influence destinies beyond you.

If you want to better understand how God values the female half of His creation, read The Divine Romance by Gene Edwards.

The point isn't that a woman's power comes only from her role as a mother. (I'm not just talking about birthin' babies.) The point is that her power definitely doesn't come from buying into Satan's lies.

Have you ever noticed that Satan's lies usually start with a grain of truth? That's how he hooks us. In the Garden of Eden he told Eve that if she ate the forbidden fruit, she would be like God—even though God had already created her in His image. She fell for the deception that she could have more power if she became a little goddess on her own.

Ladies, not much has changed. Satan still whispers lies in our ears—through feminist ideology, goddess spirituality (New Age, Wicca, witchcraft), and the sexually confused indoctrination of lesbianism. As a daughter of the feminist movement, I can tell you that I have struggled with confusion about how to reconcile the world's point of view with a biblical perspective of what it means to be a woman. And now, a whole new generation of young women is being seduced into a deceptive mass of half-truths. We don't need the feminist movement to "empower" us! As believers, we have the supernatural power of the Holy Spirit at our disposal, regardless of our gender. That, girlfriend, is all the power you will ever need.

THE POWER OF INFLUENCE

In *The Power of Femininity,* Michele McKinney defines femininity as "strength under control." Femininity, she says, is "strength wrapped in a velvet glove."

> It is an inner quality that emanates from a woman who knows her calling and her value. Feminine women are strong women because their influence is deeply felt. This influence gets beneath the surface because it is invited in. It is invited in because it is attractive and non-threatening. It is non-threatening because it doesn't seek to intimidate. You see, the feminine woman knows who she is and celebrates being all woman. She lets who she is naturally do all the work for her. The gift of influence is the invisible power that women overlook…. Because influence is a heart thing…the ability to affect the heart…. The heart is the originator of all decisions. [3]

Women have devalued the subtle power of influence. Influence can affect minds without alienating people. A woman of influence is respected because of her character and virtue. That was exactly what God needed to influence the heart of a king—not wars, not massive slaughter of lives, not pillaging and plundering, just the subtle power of the influence of a girl named Esther.

THE POWER OF A PRINCESS

Back in high school, when I was trying to find my identity by trying on everyone else's, a young man said something to me that was more profound than he ever could have known.

We met at church camp one summer. Since we lived in different cities, we began writing and seeing each other occasionally on weekends. He was different than other guys I knew, even Christian guys. He was really into the Bible, always wanted to pray, was very polite to my mom, and treated me with honor and respect. That was different. He had a way with words that was different, too, sort of poetic. One particular letter has stayed with me through the years as if it were from the very mouth of God. Along with some other Scriptures illuminating who I was in God's eyes, he included a sentence that really made me think. He wrote, "You are a princess in God's court."

He went on to expound on the precious and royal position of a princess. I had never thought of myself in such lofty ways. For days and weeks I couldn't get those words out of my mind. As I pondered them, I began to ask myself, *If I am a princess in God's court, what does that mean? How should a princess of the Most High, the King of kings, conduct herself? Is my character becoming of a princess? And what are the blessings of such a royal position? What kind of life of destiny is a princess called to live?* I was suddenly challenged to meet a higher standard. It was a wake-up call.

That sentence stuck with me long after our lives took different paths, and it continued to call out to character and a sense of destiny in me. Sadly, even though God gave me the vision early on, I didn't always live up to the standard of a princess. Like so many, I was enticed by this world. I got pulled offtrack at times, lost sight of my destiny, and suffered the pain and consequences of my mistakes.

Rise Up!

If God could use Esther and a host of other women from the Bible—not to mention countless women throughout history—to touch their generations, He can use you to touch yours. Embrace being female. As a girl, you are uniquely equipped to impact your world, your community, and your family for the kingdom of God in ways that a guy can't.

The God of all power created girl power. Ask yourself, *If I am a princess in God's court, how then should I live to bring honor to the King and be in a position to receive the blessings of royalty?* This girl thing becomes a God thing *for such a time as this.*

See It, Say It, Walk It Out

- "So God created man in his own image, in the image of God he created him; male and female he created them." (Genesis 1:27)
- "You made all the delicate, inner parts of my body and knit me together in my mother's womb. Thank you for making me so wonderfully complex! Your workmanship is marvelous—and how well I know it.... How precious are your thoughts about me, O God!" (Psalm 139:13–14, 17, NLT)
- "And afterward, I will pour out my Spirit on all people. Your sons and daughters will prophesy, your old men will dream dreams, your young men will see visions. Even on my servants, both men and women, I will pour out my Spirit in those days." (Joel 2:28–29)

Just Do It!

1. Ask your parents or the people who raised you what went through their minds when they heard the words, "It's a girl!"

2. Interview an older woman whom you admire. Ask her what she's learned in her life about the beauty of a woman. Ask her if she would be willing to be a spiritual mentor to you—to guide you in the matters of life, love, and being a woman of God (Titus 2:3–5). That's the kind of woman Darlene Sala has been to me. Don't pass up the wisdom of those who have traveled this road before you. Do a girl thing and meet her for lunch.

A Radically Pure Revolution

...forsuchatimeasthis

Then the king's personal attendants proposed,
"Let a search be made for beautiful young virgins for the king."

ESTHER 2:2

We know from the title of the book of Esther that the main character is a woman, and as we've seen, that fact is important in itself. When we meet Esther in the second chapter of the book, what is the first thing we learn about her? We learn that she is a beautiful young virgin.

I have to be honest with you. I hesitated to put this chapter so close to the beginning of the book. I didn't want you to think, *Oh, here it comes: the virginity speech.* I was afraid it would seem too heavy or even make some girls feel bad if they've already fallen short. As I thought about tacking this chapter on to the end of the book, God spoke to me: *Lisa, do you believe that My Word is divinely inspired and that every word is divinely placed?* I had to answer yes. Then it dawned on me that perhaps there's a reason that the first thing we know about Esther from the Scriptures is that she's a virgin.

So before you judge where this is going and miss the rest of Esther's incredible story, hear me out. This chapter isn't just about virginity; it's about purity. Purity of body is the result of purity of heart and mind. In fact, you can technically be a virgin and not have purity of body, heart, or mind. On the other hand, you can begin to live a life of purity now even if you aren't a virgin. Whether you are a virgin or not, it's never too early or too late to start walking in purity. This is a book about character, and sexual purity is simply a by-product of strong character.

I remember when I was younger and trying to understand my desires, emotions, and, yes, passions. I was looking for guidance and direction. Unfortunately, the message I got was short and simplistic: It's sin. It's bad. Don't do it! Nobody ever explained to me why sexual sin is so destructive or why character matters or how to walk in purity. And though the pressures were very real when I was growing up, they are even more intense today.

A SEX-CRAZED CULTURE

Sex is everywhere.

We are constantly assaulted by media messages that are unabashedly suggestive. If you buy into these messages, it seems like every young ingenue is caving in to her boyfriend's pressure or her own curiosity—or worse, feeling no pressure at all and just doing "whatever comes naturally."

Fashion has become seductive to the point that much of it is soft porn. You don't even have to buy the whole outfit anymore; the matching scarf pasted to your body is enough. (Who can forget Jennifer Lopez's "dress" at the Grammy Awards?)

And advertising, as everyone knows, uses sex to sell. All you have to do is look at the magazine display at the grocery store checkout to have your mind assaulted. Provocatively dressed women and men and shocking titles are meant to arouse your curiosity. And it works, doesn't it?

In public schools the assumption is that kids and young adults are having sex anyway, so they might as well be safe about it. The message is "It's okay as long as you don't get pregnant or pass on an STD." Schools hand out condoms, and some even show students how to use them by demonstrating on a banana. They tell students that the condom will make sex safe, and then they help girls get abortions when they find out sex isn't safe. This mind-set is leaving an entire generation of young women confused and disillusioned.

In addition to your hormones (which God created) and cultural pressures, there is a very real spiritual battle being waged over your mind, which tells your physical body what to do. I believe that the spirit of Jezebel and Delilah is telling today's young women that the way to get the attention, power, and position they want in life is by manipulating others through feminine seduction.

Jezebel was a queen. But unlike Esther, she selfishly used her power to control and manipulate other people in order to get what she wanted. In her arrogance, she painted herself up and donned her haughtiest attitude, was condescending to those she disliked, and destroyed those she hated. She practiced witchcraft *Read more* and seduced others into sexual immorality. But in the *about these two* end, did she get all that she was after? No. She was *"sisters in sin" in* sent to the dogs and experienced a violent death. *1 Kings 16–21*

Delilah was paid to use her feminine charms to *and Judges 16.* get Samson to tell her the secret of his strength. But despite his great physical strength, Samson was a weak man. Even though he was on to her scheme, this girl "worked it" (if you know what I mean) till she wore him down. Believing that she really loved him, he poured out his heart to her. Then he got a haircut and lost his source of strength; she took the money and ran. She never loved him;

she was just using him. Sounds like something you might hear about on an afternoon talk show, huh?

Even in today's permissive culture, calling a woman a "Jezebel" is a real slam on her character. Ricky Martin has a song called "Jezebel" about a woman who uses her body to tempt men and put them in compromising positions. She uses sex to get what she wants without regard for the men she leaves in her wake. The irony is that although people do not think highly of that kind of behavior, nobody does much to discourage the mentality that leads to it.

Just watch any awards show or music special. The sensual clothing and choreography seduce not only the audience but also the artists. The feeling of power that comes with sexual attention can be very addictive for a young woman who doesn't value herself.

I am ashamed to admit that it happened to me, but it did. When I was about to give up my crown as Miss California, a gown was specially designed for my final walk down the runway. When the producer of the show saw it, he said that it wasn't sexy enough. The television broadcast needed higher ratings, and he suggested that it was time for me to shed my "good girl" image. He wanted the cleavage cut to the waist and the slit of the skirt to the top of my thigh.

I was uncomfortable with his suggestions, but I was a people pleaser. I didn't value myself enough or have the confidence to say no. So the designer made the changes. To be honest, I was a little intrigued by the attention and sense of power it gave me. I still remember that final walk. The dress was a showstopper, all right, but I had crossed a line, and I knew it.

I was a professing Christian, and that dress didn't portray the elegance and integrity I wanted to be remembered for. In that instance and others like it, I compromised my character, and I later had to ask the Lord to forgive me and restore my dignity and witness.

This conflict of character is also evident in the career of Britney

Spears. The media has made a big deal about her "virginity." They wouldn't do that if their research didn't tell them that this is an important issue to a significant segment of her audience. But Britney's actions on stage and her suggestive costumes send a mixed message to girls and guys. To the girls her actions say, "You can still technically be a virgin while acting like a Jezebel." To the guys they say, "I'm the forbidden fruit. Come get me, or at least lust after me." Where's the purity? No wonder young people are confused.

Jesus talked about the importance of keeping the spirit of the law, not just the letter of the law (Matthew 23:23). I'd like to give Britney and other young artists like her the benefit of the doubt. Perhaps the success and attention she has received is so intoxicating that she doesn't even realize she's a walking contradiction and that thousands, even millions, of girls are imitating her example. Perhaps the people around her have helped her rationalize her actions and separate herself from her responsibility as a role model. I pray that she maintains her virginity, but that's not the point. She has already compromised her purity.

A RADICALLY PURE REVOLUTION

The tide is turning. There is a growing trend in today's young women toward modesty, chastity, virginity, and saving themselves for marriage. These one-time traditional values are becoming popular again. Apparently, young women are wising up to the price their parents paid during the sexual revolution. Many have experienced the devastating impact of "free love" (divorce and marital infidelity) on their own families and have learned that it didn't leave those who bought into it feeling loved, happy, or fulfilled.

Many in this generation are becoming radical for God's righteousness. They are rebelling against the status quo in this sexually charged culture and are becoming radically pure. And radical purity is about more than just your body; it's about the condition of your heart and mind.

Remember the spiritual battle we talked about? Satan wants to seduce you into the sin of impurity so he can destroy you emotionally. If he can get you to compromise, he can constantly condemn and accuse you, causing you to drown in shame. Once shame and guilt have engulfed you, your relationship with and effectiveness for God will be diminished. Fleeting moments of pleasure are not worth the cost, not to mention the baggage you will take into marriage. Trust me, that's too high a price to pay.

Young women are taking what the world considers to be radical steps. They aren't buying into the lie of instant gratification. They are going against the tide and saving the gift of intimacy to give to one person in marriage. More than a million teenagers have made the True Love Waits pledge:

"Believing that true love waits, I make a commitment to God, myself, my family, my friends, my future mate, and my future children to be sexually abstinent from this day until the day I enter a biblical marriage relationship."

AN ESTHER MOMENT

Here is one young woman's very candid letter that I found on truelovewaits.com.

Hello,

I am eighteen years old, and I lost my virginity at the age of sixteen to a guy I thought I loved. This was the biggest mistake of my life. Even though we were each other's first, I had a scare with an STD. Beware that you can get a STD even if it is the first time for both of you! I was brought up being taught that you do not have sex until you are married, but I got caught up in the moment, and let me tell you that after the first time, it gets easier and easier to do. Every time afterward, I would cry because I was so mad at myself. One of my good friends introduced me to the TRUE LOVE WAITS program and taught me what a "born-again virgin" is, and I made the commitment.

This friend has been so patient. She has been keeping me accountable for my actions (which has not been easy), and I thank her for that. Bethany, you are the best friend a person could ask for!

Even if you have had sex already, don't give up on yourself. Now that I have completely stopped everything that was leading to sex I am so much happier. I have a new outlook on life.

I encourage everyone to save yourself till you are married, and if you have already lost your virginity don't give up. Find a friend to help you stay accountable, and go for purity from this day forward!

Sara

Wow, Sara has learned a painful but very valuable lesson. Like I said, it's never too late to start walking in purity. I applaud Sara for her courage to walk in character and her willingness to be transparent and accountable.

ADVICE FROM VIRGINS

Imagine opening the newspaper one day and instead of "Ann Landers" or "Dear Abby" seeing the "Virgin Advice Column." Well, that's exactly what I have for you. Several of my friends who are in their thirties are still unmarried. They are attractive, intelligent, successful, and, yes, still virgins. How do they do it? Here is their advice:

Decide.

Make a conscious decision before the heat of the moment not to give away the gift that was given at birth until you give it to the man you marry.

Steer clear of temptation.

In *The Prayer of Jabez*, Bruce Wilkinson says:

> Without a temptation, we would not sin. Most of us face too many temptations—and therefore sin too often—because we don't ask God to lead us away from temptation. We make a huge spiritual leap forward, therefore, when we begin to focus less on beating temptation and more on avoiding it.

Don't be alone with a man in his or your house or apartment. Avoid situations that you know have the potential for temptation—both for you and for him.

Set mental boundaries.

The Bible gives the best prescription for setting boundaries to keep our minds pure:

> Finally, brothers [and sisters], whatever is true, whatever is noble, whatever is right, whatever is pure, whatever is lovely, whatever is admirable—if anything is excellent or praiseworthy—think about such things. (Philippians 4:8)

My "virgin advisors" tell me that could mean avoiding steamy romance novels and movies that can leave images that replay in your mind and arouse you. Also, excuse yourself from conversations that become sexually suggestive (Ephesians 4:29).

Set physical boundaries.

Decide how far is too far—holding hands, hugging, kissing, making out—and then put a stake in the sand that says "Do Not Pass." If you don't set physical boundaries when you are thinking clearly, you will easily cross the line in the heat of the moment. So be up front and direct with guys from the start.

Dress for pure success. Watch what you wear and how you wear it. Don't advertise the product if its not for sale.

A growing number of people have adopted the philosophy of courtship outlined by Joshua Harris in I Kissed Dating Goodbye. It's radical but not unrealistic.

Scripture. ♡

Let me say it again: The Word of God is your best weapon in a test or battle. Put the verses in the "See It, Say It, Walk It Out" section at the end of each chapter in your heart, your mind, your mouth, and even in your purse. Meditate on them day and night. Make the Word of God your constant confession.

Dating doesn't have to be combative if you're armed with Scripture. First Corinthians 13 says that love is patient. So why rush into sex? "It is not self-seeking.... Love does not delight in evil but rejoices with the truth. It always protects" (1 Corinthians 13:5–7). Any guy who tries to pressure you into sex is not patient, is most certainly self-seeking, and isn't interested in protecting you.

> "How can a young person stay pure? By obeying your word and following its rules. I have hidden your word in my 💗 heart, that I might not sin against you."
> Psalm 119:9, 11, NLT

Cultivate female friendships.

There is strength in numbers. Establish solid friendships with other young women who have made the same commitment to purity so you can encourage one another and hold one another accountable. This may mean cutting off some friendships in order to protect yourself from the pressure to compromise.

These are difficult choices, but they will protect your physical and mental purity. Your relationships with God and your future husband are worth every bit of the effort.

AN *E*STHER MOMENT

When I was in college, a young woman I'd met through pageants invited me to attend an intercampus ministry group. At one event, Dana introduced me to Tom, one of the student leaders in the group and a popular football player at USC. The sparks that went off when they were in the same room were obvious to everyone. But they didn't date or openly acknowledge their attraction as they poured themselves into ministering side by side to other students.

The Christian fellowship they were part of had adopted a philosophy of courting from Larry Tomzac's book *Why Wait till Marriage?* At that time, the purity movement was in its infancy, and it was so contrary to our dating game culture that it seemed like a cult to me. I had never heard of such a thing. Today, the radically pure revolution is gaining momentum, thanks to pioneers like Dana and Tom.

Read The Princess and the Kiss by Jennie Bishop to a little girl. It's a children's book with a big girl message.

Only after it was clear to everyone around them that God had called them to be together did they decide to court. Not too long after that I received an invitation to their wedding. It was a glorious event at the Crystal Cathedral in Garden Grove, California, with hundreds of people in attendance. It was a breathtaking moment when Dana walked down the aisle in her white dress. You could have heard a pin drop when the minister said, "Tom, you may kiss your bride." When he did, a roar of applause went up. You see, Dana and Tom's first kiss was at the altar, and everybody knew it.

What an incredible moment that was—what a statement of purity. It was "pure intimacy," starting with the first kiss. That had a powerful impact on me. It forced me to admit that I didn't have that level of purity in my own life. Dana and Tom, thank you for your witness of purity. I have never forgotten it.

GETTING BACK TO ESTHER...

Esther's situation paints a picture for us. She was a countercultural girl—a Jew—and a foreigner in the land of Persia. There were certain rules in the Jewish culture that others did not live by. There were limits on how much contact a young man and woman could have and guidelines for courtship and marriage. These rules and regulations were set up to protect the Jews, to keep them from being tainted by the culture of the pagan Persians. Esther had to maintain a standard of morality that was foreign to the culture in which she lived.

As Christians, we are also called to live as foreigners in this world, and therefore we must live, act, and think differently. We are called to be in the world but not of it. We cannot expect to walk in purity if we go along with what "everyone else" is doing. We're not called to follow the crowd!

If you want to read more about sexual purity and some practical ways to keep it, check out And the Bride Wore White: Seven Secrets to Sexual Purity *by Dannah Gresh.*

I could talk until I'm blue in the face about virginity and the "hows" and "whys" of physical purity, but there's not room in this book for that.

The point is that Esther was a virgin. Physical purity is an indication of greater character at work in the life of a young woman—purity of mind and motive. If your character is compromised in this area of your life, I guarantee that it's compromised in other areas as well.

As we'll see in the coming chapters, it was the beauty of her character—purity, obedience, honesty, courage, self-sacrifice, discipline of prayer, wisdom, humility—that set Esther apart and positioned her for the Lord's favor as a young woman of destiny.

Rise Up!

God is raising up a generation of Esthers who will stand in stark contrast to the spirit of Jezebel and join the ranks of the radically pure revolution. Generation Esther is taking on Generation Jezebel. The church is the standard by which the rest of the world is to be judged. Are you setting a standard or settling for second best? Do you want to be a woman of destiny? God is calling out to the Esther in you to rise up and walk in the character of purity *for such a time as this.*

See It, Say It, Walk It Out

"I am jealous for you with a godly jealousy. I promised you to one husband, to Christ, so that I might present you as a pure virgin to him." (2 Corinthians 11:2)

☼ "Don't let anyone look down on you because you are young, but set an example for the believers in speech, in life, in love, in faith and in purity." (1 Timothy 4:12)

☼ "It is God's will that you should be sanctified: that you should avoid sexual immorality; that each of you should learn to control his own body in a way that is holy and honorable, not in passionate lust like the heathen, who do not know God…. For God did not call us to be impure, but to live a holy life." (1 Thessalonians 4:3–5, 7)

JUST DO IT!

1. Test yourself to see how much you've come to accept the permissiveness of American culture: Watch your favorite sitcom or your favorite movie with your mother, your pastor, or your young niece. You'll notice that you don't laugh at the same jokes and that you're more sensitive to sexual innuendos.

2. 📓 Journal It: Write out your own profession of purity or use the one from True Love Waits. Make it your prayer of purity every day.

_____

_____

_____

_____

_____

_____

_____

_____

Date ___/___/___
Signature_____

Pretty Is As Pretty Does

...forsuchatimeasthis

She had to complete twelve months of beauty treatments prescribed for the women, six months with oil of myrrh and six with perfumes and cosmetics.

ESTHER 2:12

I n chapter 2, Esther was taken to the palace to compete in the ulti-mate beauty contest with the ultimate prize: The winner would become the new queen of Persia. But before she could appear before the king, Esther had to undergo an entire year of beauty treat-ments. Talk about spending too much time in the bathroom! Can you even imagine a twelve-month makeover? That's any beauty-product junkie's dream. But according to the Bible, Esther was already a natural beauty—"lovely in form and features" (Esther 2:7)—so what's up with this year of beauty treatments?

The writer of the book of Esther, who was inspired by the Holy Spirit, could have left out all the details. He could have simply told us that she became queen and then moved right to the action. But the fact is that the process of preparation was part of the action: It was to make the most of Esther's physical beauty.

This is a liberating message. Beauty, after all, was God's idea.

Just look at a flower, a rainbow, or a breathtaking sunset.

BEAUTY IN THE BALANCE

As Christian women, we sometimes get the idea that God cares only about the inner person and that enhancing our outer beauty is vain or even sinful. It can be! Solomon said, "Charm is deceitful, and beauty is vain" (Proverb 31:30, NRSV). And remember what Peter wrote?

> Don't be concerned about the outward beauty that depends on fancy hairstyles, expensive jewelry, or beautiful clothes. You should be known for the beauty that comes from within, the unfading beauty of a gentle and quiet spirit, which is so precious to God. That is the way the holy women of old made themselves beautiful. (1 Peter 3:3–5, NLT)

These verses are wonderful reminders of the value that God places on inner beauty. If we're not careful, we might think that the only way to be holy is to wear no makeup, be totally grubbed out, and pay no attention to things like health and attractiveness. But that's not what the Bible says. There's a balance.

We may find ourselves in situations where other needs become much more important than external appearance, and that's okay. But that doesn't mean there's anything godly about looking dull and drab. Ignoring your appearance doesn't produce holiness any more than wearing a sackcloth and heaping ashes on your head. (Now there's a fashion statement!)

We get in trouble when our outer appearance consumes all of our time and our thought life. Or when we begin to accept or reject ourselves—or others—solely on the basis of dress or hairstyle or makeup or weight. If we think more about how we look than how to love others, then self-image has become an idol.

In *You Are Not What You Weigh*, Lisa Bevere points out that the words *image* and *idol* are almost always interchangeable in Scripture.

And trust me: Idols are downright ugly to God.

Do you see how subtle this is? And how we need the balance that comes from God's Word? On one hand, we know that being overly conscious of our outer appearance can lead to vanity and even idolatry; on the other hand, we can go to the opposite extreme of self-condemnation and the fear that caring for our appearance is sinful.

AN *E*STHER MOMENT

To give some perspective on how inner and outer beauty need to be balanced, let me tell you a true story.

Natasha was a young, beautiful girl, the creator of a Christian underground magazine in Communist Russia. She had already been to jail once but continued her covert activities after her release. When she was arrested for the second time, her captors showed her two strikingly different photographs. In one picture, a beautiful girl who could have been a movie star or a model smiled at Natasha. The other picture showed what appeared to be an old woman, with a thin, pale face and cracked lips.

Those cracked lips smiled, though, and it was the same smile as the other picture. Could it really be the same girl? Indeed, the guards assured her, it was. And if she went to prison again, they warned her, the same would happen to her. The price was too high for Natasha, and rather than give up her looks, she turned in fifty fellow believers.

Aida was the girl in the pictures. She went to prison again and again because her love for God and His Word gave her the strength to continue her Christian activities. She was only thirty years old when she was released from her fourth prison term, but she looked at least fifty or sixty. You wouldn't have recognized her except for her striking smile, which radiated

If you want to read more stories like those of Aida and Natasha, check out Jesus Freaks by D.C. Talk and Voice of the Martyrs.

her inner beauty. Her movie star looks were gone, but her true beauty remained.

COMPETING FOR THE TITLE

In situations like those of Aida and Natasha, we must lay down anything that keeps us from standing firm. Under ordinary circumstances, though, God wants us to use and improve what He has given us.

I can relate to Esther's year of preparation. From the time I had decided to compete for the title of Miss California until the moment they slipped the crown on my head, exactly one year had passed. I had just one year—twelve short months—to get my act together. Not to mention working on my body! I wanted to be the best I could be so that, no matter what the outcome, I could move forward without regrets or "if onlys."

One of the first things I did, with the help of some professionals, was to sit down and evaluate my strengths and weaknesses in every area. With that done, I set a disciplined but realistic schedule to accomplish my goals.

If you need a complete body, mind, and spirit makeover, I recommend Sheri Rose Shepherd's books Fit for Excellence and 7 Ways to Build a Better You. She shares the same biblical principles that brought healing and freedom to me.

I was overweight and out of control mentally, emotionally, and physically. It was time for a radical change, and the pageant was the motivation God used to turn me around. I began by making a total change in my eating habits, not only for the physical benefits, but also for the mental clarity I would need. I had previously been a compulsive eater. Now, I was in the gym every day not just to "buffet my body" (1 Corinthians 9:27, NASB) for swimsuit competition (my sweet brother called me "thunder thighs"), but to bring order, discipline, and healing to a body and mind in chaos.

I worked with hair and makeup artists to determine the best colors and styles for my face shape and coloring. Then I had to learn how to do the makeup and hairstyles myself. Next came wardrobe. Again we had to determine the best colors and styles for my skin tone and body type. It didn't matter if it looked good on the model in the catalog if it didn't look good on *me*.

Then it was time to pick a song. There were a number of songs I wanted to sing because of how someone else had performed them, but I had to find my own style and be true to that. In whatever spare moments I had, I began studying the newspaper and current events. I wanted to broaden my mind and force myself to formulate opinions on various issues for the personal interview.

All in all, the competition was not about looking, being, or sounding like someone else. This was about being the best *I* could be with what God had given me.

I am grateful for the many people who patiently volunteered their time and resources to help that awkward young woman from a small town shed her clumsy cocoon and find her wings. I had never worked so hard for anything to that point in my life, but the discipline I learned and the confidence I gained has accompanied me into every situation since.

BEAUTY BALANCING ACT

Beauty is a precious resource from the hand of God. And as with any God-given gifts, Satan will push us to extremes so that we are thrown off balance and lose the ability to enjoy that gift and to use it in His service.

We're deceived into believing that the standard for beauty is dictated by super models that have been so elevated in our culture or by the latest celebrity to catch the media's eye. But God doesn't want us to reflect them; He wants us to reflect Him.

God does not want us to live in bondage of any kind.

As daughters of the King, we should not be slaves to the latest fashions and fads, but neither should we present ourselves like slobs. In his letter to the Galatians, Paul writes, "Now you are no longer a slave but God's own child. And since you are his child, everything he has belongs to you" (4:7, NLT). Remember, you are a princess in God's royal court. Just before we read in Proverbs 31:30 that "charm is deceptive, and beauty does not last," (NLT) we see in verse 22 that God's ideal woman is clothed "like royalty in gowns of finest cloth" (NLT) (which she probably found while bargain hunting in verse 18!).

We need to make the most of what God has given us. As my mother always said, "Accentuate the positive, underplay the negative." At the same time, we need to make sure there is a constant deposit of character, wisdom, perspective, and temperance—inner beauty. This is what we see in Esther throughout the rest of her book. Her inner beauty accentuates her outer beauty.

A BITTERSWEET SENSATION

True beauty requires more than just a makeover. There is a much deeper meaning to Esther's beautification treatment. Many times in Scripture you'll find that a passage has both a practical and a spiritual application. The spiritual application in this case relates to inner beauty. Esther's twelve-month beauty regimen was also a process of purification and preparation.

Esther spent six months in the House of Preparation being treated with oil of myrrh. Myrrh, which means *bitter,* is a gum resin from a plant and was very valuable. It was often used as a medicine for healing, and its application would have made Esther's skin soft, smooth, and spotless.

In the Old Testament, myrrh is the first ingredient in the recipe for the special anointing oil that was used to consecrate or purify the objects used in the tabernacle (Exodus 30:23–29). Oil is a vivid symbol of the anointing of the Holy Spirit. Objects or people had to be sanctified, consecrated, and purified to prepare them to be used in the temple for a holy purpose. On a spiritual level, Esther was being purified for a divine purpose.

Then came six months of perfume, sweet spices, and cosmetics. In Scripture our prayers and worship are referred to as sweet incense or perfume that rises up to God (Revelation 5:8). Oil and sweet spices are always used together at the altar. They are symbolic of the anointing of the Holy Spirit that comes from the time we spend in prayer and worship.

Esther's treatment—with bitter myrrh and sweet perfumes—was kind of like a spiritual mud mask. Have you ever been to a spa or seen pictures of someone having a mud facial? There is nothing pretty about the process, but it does wonders for cleaning out the pores and taking off that dead outer layer of skin so that the fresh skin underneath can shine.

Character is born out of bittersweet experiences. I have always grown spiritually as a result of the bitter times in my life that forced me to seek and rely on God. At those times, the sweetness of His presence and peace overtakes me. There is nothing more beautiful than the glow of God's glory on the face of a handmaiden who has spent time in the presence of the Lord. Remember Aida, the modern-day Esther? The beauty of her smile, which remained through all the hardships of imprisonment, was all the sweeter because of the bitterness.

True beauty, the kind that comes from God, is a process that requires both bitterness and sweetness. A friend of mine once told me about a time when, as children, she and her sister raided the pantry after her mother had stocked it for her Christmas baking. They thought they had hit the jackpot when they found a large bar of Hershey's chocolate. My friend quickly stuffed as much chocolate into her mouth as she could hold—but a few seconds later it all came spewing out.

Turns out that it was bitter baking chocolate. When mixed with sweet ingredients, the bitter chocolate turns into a savory sensation, but by itself…ugh!

God's Flower Garden

No beauty comes without struggle—not even the simple beauty of a flower.

As a little girl, I remember admiring my mother's garden. There was always something in bloom around our historic home. Sometimes my mother just had to get her hands in the dirt, and I loved getting in there with her. She especially enjoyed the annual ritual of planting bulbs in the fall in anticipation of enjoying their fragrant blooms in the spring.

We spent hours and hours "turning the dirt," as she called it, and working in the mulch and compost she had faithfully prepared. It would make for fertile ground, she told me. Impatient, I wanted to just dig a hole and shove the bulb in. But no. She insisted that we prepare the soil to give the bulbs good food for the long winter.

Then she would carefully dig a hole just the right depth for each bulb. Little did I know at the time that she was teaching me a life lesson about how a woman's beauty blossoms. She explained that the beauty of the bloom was latent in the bulb. If the bulb was placed too deep, it would have to struggle too hard to get to the surface, which could limit its potential to bloom. If it was placed too close to the surface, it would not have a firm enough foundation for the stem to support the weight of the blossom: It wouldn't struggle enough, and it would pop out of the ground and bloom prematurely, only to have its beauty quickly fade.

Every day I would eagerly check the flowerbeds to see if the plants were popping out of the ground. I expected them to bloom any day. I wanted the beauty without the growth process. When that didn't happen, I forgot all about the bulbs, and the bitter cold winter passed with no sign of growth or movement.

Then one day, when winter had turned to spring, a green bud pushed through the dirt—and then another, and another. It now seemed like nothing could keep the stems from drawing their strength from the sun and soil and reaching higher each day. I could hardly stand it. A few days more and suddenly the garden burst into full bloom. The vibrant colors that had been hidden in the bulbs for so long finally appeared.

God is the great Gardener. He knows exactly what kind of soil preparation we need. He knows how deeply we need to be planted and just how much struggle will make us strong enough to hold the weight and beauty of the bloom He has placed in us, waiting to burst forth in due season. But most of all, He knows the potential that's packed in our little "bulb" before any growth takes place at all. He sees the beauty that's there because He made each of us uniquely beautiful.

Rise Up!

Discover and embrace your God-given beauty. In God's eyes you are "all that and a bag of chips." But most of all, cultivate the inner character and confidence born out of an intimate relationship with God. Submit yourself to God's beautification process that you might be consecrated for His holy purpose *for such a time as this.*

See It, Say It, Walk It Out

- "The LORD does not look at the things man looks at. Man looks at the outward appearance, but the LORD looks at the heart." (1 Samuel 16:7)
- "To bestow on them a crown of beauty instead of ashes, the oil of gladness instead of mourning, and a garment of praise instead of a spirit of despair." (Isaiah 61:3)

☼ "Like a gold ring in a pig's snout is a beautiful woman who shows no discretion." (Proverbs 11:22)

JUST DO IT!

1. Inner Beauty
   Describe a difficult experience in your life and the beautiful character that has come from it (e.g., wisdom, courage, compassion, tenderness, deeper reliance on God).

   _____

   _____

   _____

   _____

   _____

   _____

2. Outer Beauty
   Have a makeover party. Contact BeautiControl® (check out their website at www.beauticontrol.com). To find a consultant in your area contact Sharon B. Davis, National Image Trainer, at 1-800-765-8051 or e-mail your request to www.beautipage.com/beautidr. Request a Personal Image Profile®. You'll discover the right colors for your skin, suggested makeup and hairstyles for your face shape, and clothing for your body type—and you'll have a blast. Be sure to request a product brochure for the youth line of makeup as well. This is the cosmetic line I use on the 700 Club. Don't waste time and money like I did for years. This company has great products at reasonable prices founded by a wonderful Christian woman, Jinger Heath.

 Set Apart

...forsuchatimeasthis

*And [Hegai] moved her and her maidservants
to the best place in the house of the women.*

ESTHER 2:9, NKJV

T he author of the book of Esther, traditionally thought to be Mordecai, doesn't give us much insight into how Esther feels as her story unfolds. Much like a reporter, he just gives the facts. But as women, we'd love to know a little bit more.

We want to know, "How did that make you *feel,* Esther? What was going on inside your heart?" We want to know the colors, the smells, the music playing in the background, the ambience. We're curious to know what everyone said.

By God's design, females are sensory beings. Yet in this little book of Esther, one of only two books in the Bible called by a woman's name, we are left to impose our own female instincts on the scenario. So we ask ourselves, "How would *I* feel?"

Today, the exotic setting of Esther 2 may not be that easy for us to visualize. The best comparison might be to some sort of beauty pageant, where contestants come together and stay in a swank hotel, usually buddying up and sharing a room. For a few stressful, exciting days, they get bussed to special events in the host city, photographers click-ing away at every opportunity.

Then each contestant competes in the interview, talent, evening gown, and swimsuit categories. The judges pick a winner, crown her, load her up with gifts and perks, and send her off to the next level of competition. The rest of the contestants return to their former lives amid familiar surroundings of family and friends, school and work, home and church. In short, they pick up where they left off.

Life goes on.

That wasn't the case in the Miss Persia Pageant. In that culture, hundreds—perhaps even thousands—of attractive teenage virgins were plucked from their homes and families, *never to return again*. Most of the girls had probably never been away from home before, and all of them were strangers to the palace, its ways, and its people.

What awaited these young women was not as glamorous as we might imagine. The prestige of living in the royal palace was no com-pensation for life as royal mistresses. Only one young lady would be queen. The rest would basically be prisoners in the female quarters of the palace for the rest of their lives, with no chance for love, families, or lives of their own.

In *The Wizard of Oz*, Dorothy just had to click her ruby slippers together three times and repeat "There's no place like home," and she was back in Kansas, but there was no going home for these girls.

Even so, they had one another. You know how girls are. We typi-cally run in packs. We can't even go to the restroom by ourselves. Out of insecurity, the girls would probably have wanted to hang together as they settled into their new home away from home.

But put yourself in Esther's shoes. She might well have been the only Jew surrounded by pagans. Most likely she had no one with whom she could share her faith, customs, and nationality—the things closest to her heart.

Esther 2:8–9 tells us that Esther was housed in her own private quarters, which further separated her from the rest of that bevy of beauties. You can easily imagine her questions: Why had Hegai placed her in a suite by herself? Sure, it was a nice place, but how terribly alone and afraid she must have felt! She may have been a person of destiny, but she was still just a young girl, subject to all the usual human emotions.

To make things worse, Hegai gave her all sorts of preferential treatment—special attention, food, cosmetics—which probably didn't win her any points with the other girls. Favor may be from God, but that doesn't mean that everybody will be happy for you. Jealousy is a powerful emotion, and it may have further isolated Esther from the other young women. (It was probably a good thing she did have her own room!)

THE BEST PLACE

The Bible says that Esther was taken to "the best place" for the women. As we think about being set apart, we don't always see such separation as a good thing—much less "the best place." Sometimes the best place is a hard place to be.

If you remember, Esther was set apart because of her sexual purity. As a Jew she was already set apart as one of God's chosen people. She was not just being prepared to become the queen, as she might have thought. She was being purified to be God's divine instrument to save the Jewish people. She was set part for a holy purpose.

In the Bible the phrase *set apart* is used synonymously with other words like *sanctification, consecration, purification,* and *holiness.* People and things used in the temple were set apart—purified and consecrated—for that holy purpose of worship. An entire tribe of people, the Levites, were set apart and made holy before they could go into the temple or touch the objects used to perform sacrifices.

Our human nature often rebels against the perceived constraints, boundaries, or disciplines of being set apart. But we have to remind ourselves that God sees the big picture. He loves us, and He knows what He's doing. When God sets us apart, He is bringing us to the *best place*. As with Esther, God sets us apart for a purpose—for preparation, purification, and prayer.

God knows what it will take for us to be spiritually ready for what is ahead. He knows what's around the next bend. A season of being set apart might not be at all what we think it is. It might be about something much bigger than we could have dreamed. Don't fight it! *Embrace* it so you'll be rich in character when the King calls.

Are you getting the picture? When you're set apart, you're sanctified, consecrated, and made holy for God's purpose and pleasure. When you choose to be set apart, you are choosing a lifestyle that will glorify Him. You will be distinct from the rest of the world. You will be different.

Get used to it!

Different, Not Weird

I was raised in a Christian family, and I asked Jesus into my heart when I was just five years old. Growing up, I didn't smoke, drink, take drugs, swear, sleep around, or hang out with those who did. I went to church on Sunday mornings, Sunday nights, and Wednesday nights; I participated in youth group, choir, and mission trips. If it was happening at church, I was there. It was a great way to grow up.

But as I got older, I noticed that not everyone had been raised like me. I was different. I began to wonder why I was different. Why couldn't I participate in some of the activities that others seemed to enjoy so much? I began to feel like I was being laughed at and joked about. I wondered if I was missing something.

One night while I was in college, there was a postgame party that all the popular athletes, cheerleaders, and other party people were going to. I was a cheerleader, but I rarely attended those events because I wasn't a party girl.

But it was college and I was curious. It was that time in life when you're trying to figure out if you're really that sweet girl your parents raised or if you're her evil alter ego anxious to escape. Perhaps it was time to ditch my clean image and take a walk on the wild side. After all, I was on my own. My parents weren't there to tell me that I couldn't go. Maybe it was time to find out what I was missing.

Oh, did I mention that there was *a guy?*

There's always *a guy.*

Well, *this* guy didn't even know I existed, but I knew he was going to be at that party. Apprehensive but tingling from the adrenaline, I worked up the courage to go in.

I knew plenty of people there, yet I felt very out of place. I wasn't quite sure how to act. Certain that everyone could see my awkwardness, I joined the other partygoers; I grabbed a beer. I don't think I even drank any; I just held it. The *guy* was surrounded by fans and friends, and there was no way I was going to try to penetrate that wall of people just to say "hi" with a goofy look on my face. I kept trying to look cool and act nonchalant, but I wasn't very good at it. I kept asking myself, *What am I doing here?*

Then I heard the voice of one of the guys at the party, a guard on the football team: "Lisa, what are *you* doing here?" His question caught me off guard (pardon the pun). I wasn't sure how to respond. He was a nice guy, and I could tell he wasn't being mean-spirited. He just looked perplexed. Then, like a big brother, he sat me down and said, "Lisa, you don't belong here." He asked if I had my car or if I needed a ride home. He walked me out and I left—just like that.

In that moment, I heard God's voice through that young man: *Lisa, you have been set apart. You are special. I have not called you to this party life. And if this is where the guy you're attracted to is, he's not for you.* God was looking out for me.

Looking back, I realize that I needed to understand who I was as a child of God and His destiny for my life. Remember that if you are a princess in God's court, you are different, and your actions should match your privileged position.

Was I an angel from that time on? No. Did I venture out on the edge again in search of my own identity and purpose in life? Yes. Did I make mistakes? Yes. But that experience served as a reminder that God had a plan for my life that required me to be different—to be set apart.

Being set apart can be hard for young women who many times are pleasers. Too often, that's how we obtain our sense of self-worth and feeling of belonging. Being set apart for God may require you not to go along with the crowd. You may have to step away from the herd mentality and stand alone. But don't worry; you won't be alone for long. The key to being content is the confidence that God is your source of approval, your place of belonging. The Holy Spirit will give you that confidence. And if you are faithful to God, He will provide you with friends who will stand by you and hold you accountable, friends who will love you in the tough times.

Be encouraged. You are not alone. There are others who are also choosing to be set apart. You are part of a great army of Esthers that is rising up to say, "We are not ashamed of the gospel of Jesus Christ. If God is for us, then who can be against us?"

An *Esther* Moment

Recently I corresponded by e-mail with a young "Esther" I've known for a few years. Dana Elizabeth is a young lady of character, a diligent student, and a dedicated musician who is respected by her peers and elders. She baby-sat my daughters one summer and taught them piano. She recently went off to college on a music scholarship. At only seventeen, she is a freshman away from family and friends for the first time. As you might expect, the first few days and weeks were full of anxiety, fear, and loneliness. Phone calls and e-mails were her lifeline.

Doubts plagued her. *Had she done the right thing? Had she truly heard God's call? Was she in the right place?*

Despite her anxiety, Dana Elizabeth has a growing sense of deep-down confidence that God is setting her apart for this season of life to further prepare her for the calling of music. She has set herself apart as a young Christian woman and has devoted this time in her life to develop her God-given gifts. I have no doubt that she will be successful. If you pass her on campus, you'll see that she has the mantle of Esther *for such a time as this.*

And so do you if you choose to be set apart.

ANOTHER *E*STHER MOMENT

As her friends made plans for college and career, Kristina, quiet and shy, was still unsure of her calling, her purpose, her passion. She had no direction, no sense of destiny. What she did have was a burden for her generation and a desire to know God in a deeper way. As she pondered this pivotal time in her life and the kind of young woman she desired to become, she thought of several young ladies of godly character who had invested in her life when she was younger. These young role models all had something in common—a passion for God—and they had all attended a one-year discipleship program called Master's Commission. So Kristina decided to set apart the next year of her life to seek the Master.

I highly recommend: *Master's Commission: A Generational Call to Character* 2810 N. Park Rd. Spokane, WA 99262 509-926-8450 www.masterscommission.org Directors, Terry and Deborah Dawes Email: mc@victoryfaith.org

During twelve months of intense Bible study that focused on building personal Christian character, Kristina began to feel an overwhelming desire to dream, and dream big, for her destiny. She became fascinated with politics and restoring godly moral foundations in our country for *her* generation. At about that same time God brought her to the attention of the organizers of The Call, a rally that gathered on the Mall in Washington, D.C., on September 2, 2000. That's where I first saw Kristina.

As I watched the television coverage of this event, I was speechless at the passion and conviction of this unassuming young woman. She cried out to God in repentance for her generation before a huge crowd. The powerful conclusion came as she led her peers in the prayer that they had never been allowed to pray, the prayer that was removed from the classrooms of our public schools in 1962:

> "Almighty God, we acknowledge our dependence on You and beg
> Your mercy on us, our parents, our teachers, and our nation."

This quiet girl was positioned to boldly impact her generation, and she continues to do so because she was obedient to be set apart for preparation. Just think of what God might do through you if you choose to be set apart.

AN OASIS IN THE DESERT

Being set apart in the *best place* might be like an oasis in the desert or a calm in the middle of a storm. In all the hustle and bustle of getting ready for the biggest event of her life, God gave Esther a quiet place where she could close her eyes and be still. While everyone else was vying for a turn in the bathroom, Esther was in the calm of her own space. In fact, she was in the best place in the palace with seven choice maidens to help her.

Can't you just see it? In one wing of the palace, all the women were frantic, scurrying around trying to find lost shoes, screaming for nail polish to fix runs in pantyhose, trying to fix busted zippers on new gowns.

And then there was Esther…a soft song on her lips as she listened to praise music on her headphones. Maybe she took time for a morning run, while dew still clung to the grass. While toning her body, she stirred up her spiritual gifts through prayer and reciting Scriptures. As she breathed in the strength of the Lord and prepared herself for the coming event, she was confident and at peace. Chaos may have surrounded her, but she was settled in her spirit because she had spent time in the best place.

You realize, of course, that I am having a little fun with the text. But Esther's best place is a picture of the sanctuary God has prepared for us when we answer the call to come away and be set apart.

Being set apart might be something as simple as disciplining yourself for a daily devotional time, a sweet, quiet, intimate time with the Lord. You don't have to go to some fancy retreat. Your quiet place for prayer and Bible study might be as close as your bedroom. If you don't know how to get started, buy a daily devotional from a Christian bookstore. While you're there, pick up a praise tape. Even simpler, just start reading the Bible, and pray that God will speak to you through it.

I like to take power prayer walks. I walk hard and pray hard. Afterward, my mind is clear, my body is rejuvenated, and my spirit is renewed. I usually hear God's voice giving me fresh insights for the day.

Have you sensed God asking you to set apart a summer or vacation time to take a mission trip? I know many young people who have had a radical encounter with God while on a short-term, cross-cultural trip.

Perhaps God is tugging on your heart to set apart a year of your formal education and participate in an in-depth Bible study or discipleship/training program. I wish I'd been obedient to that tugging, but I didn't think I could "afford" to take the time away from my career track. How foolish and shortsighted of me!

What kind of preparation will you need for the destiny God has for you? You might have to be set apart for a season of special training or college. It might require sacrifice and courage to leave home, family, and friends. Being set apart isn't always easy…but you can be sure that God is with you.

Whether it is for practical preparation or spiritual preparation, don't let fear or apathy distract you from stepping out and being set apart.

RISE UP!

Join the ranks of other Esthers who have been set apart for a holy purpose. As a child of God, you are called to be in the world but not of it. You are a peculiar people, a holy nation. Spend time in God's presence daily to know His peace and purpose in your life. Choose to be set apart in body, mind, and spirit *for such a time as this.*

SEE IT, SAY IT, WALK IT OUT

- "Before I formed you in the womb I knew you, before you were born I set you apart." (Jeremiah 1:5)
- "Therefore come out from them and be separate, says the Lord. Touch no unclean thing, and I will receive you….
  Since we have these promises, dear friends, let us purify ourselves from everything that contaminates body and spirit, perfecting holiness out of reverence for God." (2 Corinthians 6:17; 7:1)
- "Know that the LORD has set apart the godly for himself." (Psalm 4:3)

JUST DO IT!

1. Journal It:
   Evaluate yourself. As a Christian, are you set apart in your actions and lifestyle? Be honest with yourself. Have the courage to ask God to reveal any area of your life that is not set apart or might be compromising your position as a daughter of the King.

_____

_____

_____

2. Set apart a daily devotional time for at least a week. Begin to journal what God speaks to your heart during this time through His Word and through prayer.

3. Pray about taking a mission trip. It will radically change your life. Contact any of these organizations for details.

YOUNG LIFE

P.O. Box 520
Colorado Springs, Colorado 80901
719-381-1800
www.younglife.org

YOUTH WITH A MISSION, INTERNATIONAL

YWAM-SMC
P.O. Box 8503
Madison, Wisconsin 53708
888-595-2542
SMC@haystack.org
www.ywam.org

TEEN MANIA MINISTRIES

22392 FM 16 W.
Lindale, Texas 75771
800-229-8336
info@teenmania.org
www.teenmania.org

INTERVARSITY CHRISTIAN FELLOWSHIP/USA

P.O. Box 7895
Madison, Wisconsin 53707-7895
608-274-4823 ext. 346
eseaberg@ivcf.org

chapter five

Friendship

He also assigned her seven maids specially chosen from the king's palace.

ESTHER 2:9, NKJV

When we last saw Esther, she had moved into special quarters for her year of preparation. This arrangement separated her—at least to some extent—from the rest of the girls. But God in His grace and mercy didn't leave her isolated.

God created women to be *relational*. Never doubt it! In fact, it's been demonstrated that the average woman uses twice as many words in a given day than the average guy. (Big surprise, huh?) That's why we need girlfriends. We need someone to share things with. We like to talk it out. Our wise Creator understands our need for female friendships, and here we see how He provided true and loyal friends for Esther during one of the most difficult seasons of her life.

SEVEN STEADFAST MAIDENS

Separated from her loving, adoptive father, Mordecai, Esther was dropped into strange surroundings in the company of women who may or may not have been a good influence on her. Perhaps by setting Esther apart, God was protecting her from the whole competitive atmosphere. (You know how girls can get.) Esther may not have been aware that she was in a destiny-preparation mode, but God knew. And working through Hegai, He handpicked a circle of steadfast companions for her.

Between the time the maidservants were first assigned to Esther and the time they stood beside her during her crisis, several years passed—at least two or three, but perhaps even more than ten. During that time, these women learned a lot about one another, and it's likely that the seven maidens may have learned Esther's secret: She was a Jew.

The maidservants could have used this information against Esther—perhaps in an effort to better their own position in the palace or with the king. But did any of them betray her? No, not one. As it turned out, far from being fair-weather chums, they were solid and faithful friends. In Esther's time of crisis, they joined with her to fast and pray for her wisdom, direction, and protection. And while they were at it, they took on her burden for her people. They were fasting and praying to the God of Israel.

This tells us a lot about Esther. When you were going through the fickleness of young friendships, your mother probably told you: "To have a friend, you need to be a friend." Esther must have been a friend for these women to be so loyal to her.

I believe that Esther's experience is an example of what God does for us sometimes during crucial periods in our lives. He separates us from negative influences that might hinder us or drag us down and brings into our lives loyal companions that will help us as we prepare to serve the King. By the same token, He wants us to be the kind of friend that will help others fulfill their destiny in the kingdom.

FRIENDS IN NEED

The power of friendship, for good or for evil, is great. Friends have a tremendous impact on one another's thoughts, actions, and life choices.

During the identity-shaping years and throughout life, our friends and family help us figure out who we are, even as we shape and influence others.

To a great extent we discover ourselves—our identity—through the feedback we get from friends and family. Through the eyes of others, we discover who we are. Friends act as a mirror or reflection of who we are becoming. We begin to define ourselves and adjust the focus of our self-image from our interaction with others.

In other words, you become who you hang with. It has been said, "Show me who your friends are, and I will show you who you will become." That's why hanging with the right people is so critical. Solomon wrote, "He who walks with the wise grows wise, but a companion of fools suffers harm" (Proverbs 13:20). The apostle Paul stated it rather bluntly: "Do not be misled: Bad company corrupts good character" (1 Corinthians 15:33).

I believe that friendships are providential. In other words, God is intimately involved in the "when" and "where" and "who" of our lives. He knows better than we do who will help us become who He wants us to be. And remember, it may not be the prettiest or most popular girl who will be the best companion for you. This can be a hard lesson to learn.

I remember vividly my first day of junior high. A cute, quirky girl named Maria sat next to me in homeroom. As we talked, we realized that we had lived just down the street from each other our entire lives. I had gone to public school, and she had gone to private, so we hadn't ever met. We were as different as night and day, but we became fast friends that year. We shared silly times and sad times together, and we became inseparable.

As it turned out, Maria, whom I had providentially met only two months earlier, was there for me when my eighteen-year-old brother, Jimmy, was killed in a small-plane crash. I was just thirteen, and I was absolutely devastated by the loss.

More than just an older brother, Jimmy had been my mentor and best friend. He'd been my source of strength during our parents' divorce when I was nine years old. He'd looked out for me since we were little kids. He'd included me in everything. Whatever he was doing, I was there.

But now he was gone, and I didn't know how to "be." My friendship with Maria helped me through that dark and terrible time. God had known that I would need her. I had no idea then that more hard times were ahead for me.

When we went on to high school, I became involved in activities that put me in a new circle of friends, and I didn't see Maria as much. Then, when I was seventeen, Mom and I had to move from the big house I had lived in since childhood. That triggered a totally unexpected crisis.

I began to feel depressed and to withdraw from people. Years of deep emotional pain from my parents' divorce and my brother's death began to surface. It wasn't long before I developed an eating disorder, which only intensified my pain and insecurity. During those hard times, other friends pulled away from me. They just couldn't understand what was going on in my life, and they backed off.

But Maria—sweet, exuberant, loyal Maria—stuck with me. Others came and went, but she remained. And to this day, she's more than just a friend; she's like a sister. A godly friend can be a divine instrument in your life, either by word or by example. A God-appointed friend can bring comfort, good counsel, encouragement, conviction. She can provide a safe place where you can be vulnerable and share secret fears and dreams. Through personal experience, I have proved the words of Ecclesiastes 4:9–10 in my own life:

Two are better than one,
because they have a good return for their work:
If one falls down, his friend can help him up.

But pity the man who falls
and has no one to help him up!

FRIENDS INDEED

A good Christian friend will also hold your feet to the fire! Because she loves you and knows you are called to be set apart for Jesus Christ, she will risk even your rejection to speak the truth in love and confront you in an area of carelessness or compromise in your life. I think that's what the author of Hebrews was talking about when he wrote: "Let us consider how we may spur one another on toward love and good deeds" (Hebrews 10:24–25). Solomon meant pretty much the same thing when he wrote, "You use steel to sharpen steel, and one friend sharpens another" (Proverbs 27:17, *The Message*).

We all need a friend like that at times.

My friend Kim can speak a word or conduct herself in a way that calls me to a higher standard. She never does it in an obvious, self-righteous way. In fact, most of the time she's not even aware of how God has spoken through her words or actions.

There was one instance when I had finally gotten a TV movie role that was a big enough billing for me to be included in the closing credits. I was so excited; I called all my friends and family and told them to watch. Just seeing my name in the credits—you'd have thought I'd won an Oscar. I was on cloud nine. A few days later I got the most beautiful card from Kim. I always enjoy getting a card or letter from her. She has a way of wrapping the gift of encouragement in an envelope. This time was no different.

Laced with Scripture and smiley faces, the note praised my accomplishment. But the words that followed came directly from heaven: "Lisa, how great it was to see your name in the credits, but how much more wonderful it is to know that your name is written in the Lamb's Book of Life."

That one line stopped me in my tracks and challenged me to evaluate my priorities. It was like getting an adjustment from a spiritual chiropractor. Her walk and her words through the years have quietly called out the Esther in me on many occasions. She has influenced the woman I have become. That's the power of a friend.

AN *E*STHER MOMENT

From the journal of a modern-day Esther:

In the silence
of space
and time
a friend
has found
my heart
and made
a resting place

In the movement
of dance
and music
a friend
has found
my vision
and watched
dreams
become
reality

In the voice
of prayer
and fasting
a friend
has found
my purpose
and reverenced
in the
simple
revelation

—Lisa Dauffenbach[4]

BAD COMPANY

On the flip side, an alliance with an ungodly friend can often lead you to question yourself and your values. This kind of friend might leave you feeling insecure or unsettled after you've spent time together. Perhaps she opens up a whole new world to you that seems exciting yet forbidden. She may begin to subtly criticize you—the way you act, the way you dress, or the values you've held to all your life. This kind of friend can take on many faces. Maybe she is a good actress and is nice to everyone on the outside but is full of spite, manipulation, and rebellion on the inside. Such a person may trick you at first, but don't fool yourself by thinking that you can change her.

Paul's strong words to the Galatians warn of the dangers of friendships with people like that:

You were getting along so well. Who has interfered with you to hold you back from following the truth? It certainly isn't God, for he is the one who called you to freedom. But it takes only one wrong person among you to infect all the others—a little yeast spreads quickly through the whole batch of dough! (Galatians 5:7–9, NLT)

I'm not saying that we should be isolated in little holy cliques and not reach out to non-Christians. In fact, Jesus said that we are to be salt and light in the world—like a city on a hilltop at twilight. But God does warn us about making unbelievers close confidants in our inner circle—and we should certainly take note if they become the majority of our friends. These are not the people from whom we should seek counsel. The apostle Paul is very clear on that score:

Don't team up with those who are unbelievers. How can goodness be a partner with wickedness? How can light live with darkness? What harmony can there be between Christ and the Devil? How can a believer be a partner with an unbeliever? (2 Corinthians 6:14–15, NLT)

In other words, you may have to carefully evaluate your relationships. Look at each relationship and ask yourself, *Is this a maiden friend, a mission field, or a minefield?*

- If she's a *minefield,* do just what you'd do if you encountered a real minefield in a war zone. Back away very carefully, watching where you step.
- If she's a *mission field,* enlist other Christian friends to pray with you for this individual. But don't let yourself become discolored or ensnared by cynical or ungodly attitudes.

☀ If she's a *maiden friend* like Esther's seven loyal companions,
thank the Lord for His mercy and grace.

In the process of evaluating your friendships, make sure that you're a maiden friend yourself. You wouldn't want your friends to read this and decide that they need to reconsider their friendship with you! God wants to put you in a position to be a choice maiden—a God-appointed friend—for someone else. All that you desire in a friend must be true of you as well. What was it Jesus said? "Give, and it will be given to you. A good measure, pressed down, shaken together and running over, will be poured into your lap. For with the measure you use, it will be measured to you" (Luke 6:38).

TRUE FRIENDS ARE FEW

God gave Esther seven strong friends in her time of transition and need. If you find seven such friends in a *lifetime,* you are blessed.

Don't be so insecure that you have to have lots of friends in order to feel good about yourself. Needing to be liked in order to fill an emptiness or void in your life may lead you to compromise just to be accepted. Do you freak out if you think someone doesn't like you? If you are set apart like we talked about in the last chapter, then become comfortable with not being liked by everyone. Some may even be against you if you are strong and sincere about your faith.

I have felt the sting of that kind of rejection myself. I have also anguished in the humbling realization of my own need to be liked. Those are painful lessons, but don't let them get you down. There are other Esthers out there just like you. No matter how many friends you have, remember that your ultimate security and identity comes from Christ, not the crowd.

RISE UP!

What kind of friend are you? Do you offer your friends the kind of comfortable intimacy that makes them feel that they can be themselves? Are you the kind of friend who gives godly counsel when it's needed—but also takes it in the spirit it's intended when offered to you? Do you choose friends based on the social position they give you, or based on genuine companionship, loyalty, and integrity? If you are a "choice maiden" to your friend, you will have that kind of friend to lean on when you need her.

Friendships matter, *for such a time as this.*

SEE IT, SAY IT, WALK IT OUT

- ♥ "A friend is always loyal, and a brother is born to help in time of need." (Proverbs 17:17, NLT)
- ♥ "A [woman] of many companions may come to ruin, but there is a friend who sticks closer than a [sister]." (Proverbs 18:24)
- ♥ "Perfume and incense bring joy to the heart, and the pleasantness of one's friend springs from his earnest counsel." (Proverbs 27:9)

JUST DO IT!

1. Try this friendship formula from my own paraphrase of the famous "love chapter"—1 Corinthians 13 (adapted from NLT, emphasis mine). Copy this verse and keep it in your Bible or someplace where you will see it regularly:

Friendship is very patient and kind, never jealous or envious, never boastful or proud, never haughty or selfish or rude. *Friendship* does not demand its own way. It is not irritable or touchy. It does not hold grudges and will hardly even notice when others do it wrong. If you love someone [as a friend], you will be loyal to her no matter what the cost. You will always believe in her, always expect the best of her, and always stand your ground in defending her. *The love of a godly friend...*endures through every circumstance.

Now that's a friend. But remember, to have a friend like that you must also be a friend like that.

The Blessings of Obedience

...forsuchatimeasthis

*For Esther obeyed the command of Mordecai
as when she was brought up by him.*

ESTHER 2:20, NKJV

Remember my fear about how you would react to the "virginity speech"? Well, here's another one that many of us dread. It's the honor-thy-father-and-mother speech—the submit-to-authority speech. Ugh.

As I was writing this chapter, I tried to figure out how I could be politically correct—maybe use less offensive words. I found myself looking up synonyms for words like *obey* and *submit*. But in the end, the Lord wouldn't let me do it. The more I thought and prayed about it, the more I came to understand that obedience is the key to experiencing the full blessing of God.

Now, before your shoulders slump...before you roll your eyes...before you decide to skip this chapter—*stop!* Give me a minute or two to put this in perspective for you.

A friend of mine once told me about his first plane ride in a small prop plane. As the plane circled over his hometown, he began to recognize landmarks, and soon he was able to pick out the street where he lived. He found it strange to look down at the streets and schools and vacant lots where he'd played hide-and-seek, mastered riding a bike, walked his girlfriend home from school, and learned to drive. All of it had taken place in such a *tiny* little area! It was a dramatic change of perspective for him, one that helped him see that his problems—which had seemed so huge to him—were really pretty small in the whole scheme of things.

That's what I'd like to do with this subject. Rather than focus on the suffocating obligations commonly associated with the idea of obedience, I'd like to get up in the air a couple thousand feet and give you a change of perspective. I'd like to take you on an airplane ride and show you a bigger picture than the one you've seen in the past.

I want you to take note of something significant. If you go back and look at the table of contents, you'll notice that this chapter on obedience comes *before* the chapter on favor. That's part of God's divine order. Obedience always precedes favor. Favor is one of the blessings of obedience. A rare beauty is born out of the biblical mandate of obedience and the promise of blessings to follow. And once again, Esther is our shining example. Obedience was a character trait that Esther carried with her when she left home and entered her new life in the palace.

LITTLE ORPHAN ESTHER

Esther was an orphan. Sometime in her childhood, her mother and father died.

Did she have any memories of them? Were they killed in some kind of an accident? Were they wiped out by some disease that swept through the land? This is one of those times when we'd like a little more information than the Bible gives us, but it doesn't mention Esther's parents.

Neither does it mention siblings. Very possibly, Esther was the only child left in her family. That would be a desolate feeling, wouldn't it?

No mom or dad. No brothers or sisters. No encouraging family circle. This experience alone could have been enough to leave this young woman emotionally wounded.

If Esther were alive today, she would probably be heavy into counseling! Some psychologist would be helping her unravel her unresolved feelings of rejection and fear of abandonment. Right? People would understand her inability to commit to relationships and her overall distrust of authority figures. We all know at least one person who considers herself the victim of a troubled childhood. But it's a strange thing: Esther doesn't seem messed up at all.

Esther might not have had a mom or dad, but she did have Mordecai. As a matter of fact, one of the most touching elements of this whole story is the bond between Esther and her cousin. Mordecai had adopted her into his family and raised her as his own daughter. Even after she was taken to the palace, he came by the courtyard of the harem every day to check on her—to catch a glimpse of the young woman who had become as dear as a daughter to him. Later, he even managed to get a job as a palace official, probably just to keep in touch with her. But here's the part I really want you to see: Much of Esther's great beauty is born out of her relationship with the man who had become like a father to her.

THE CHARACTER OF THE RELATIONSHIP

Esther's character throughout this book flows out of her relationship with Mordecai. Although she couldn't have realized it at the time, her preparation to be queen over a great empire began with a trusting relationship with her adoptive father.

Remember what it says in Esther 2:20?

But Esther had kept secret her family background and nationality just as Mordecai had told her to do, for she continued to follow Mordecai's instructions as she had done when he was bringing her up.

Esther obeyed Mordecai's commands, just as she had since she was a child living in his home. This passage makes it clear that Esther's character and willingness to obey didn't just suddenly appear one day. No, she had honored and obeyed Mordecai for *years*. She had deliberately chosen to make honor and obedience a part of her lifestyle.

Esther's obedience was never more essential than at the critical point in her life when Mordecai warned her to conceal her nationality and family background. He may not have had the opportunity to explain himself, but he didn't have to spend valuable time convincing her that his instructions were important. He knew she wouldn't waste time arguing. He knew that she wouldn't say to herself, *What could Mordecai possibly know about this experience? He's out of his element!* Mordecai was confident that he could trust her to follow his guidance and that she would be (here's that awful word again) obedient.

Esther's submission wasn't just lip service, either. A person can submit—outwardly, at least—without a heart or attitude of respect. You've seen it a thousand times, haven't you? A friend answers her mom politely and then makes a face when she leaves the room. Or someone speaks respectfully to the boss and then rips on him when he's out of sight. These people may be complying on the outside, but they're rebelling on the inside, thinking that they know better and that those in leadership are just trying to take the fun out of life or control them.

It's like the story of a little girl who threw a temper tantrum and had to take a time-out. Her mother told her to sit in the corner and think about what she had done. Though at first the girl refused to comply, eventually she went to the corner and sat in the chair. As the timer clicked away the five-minute sentence, the little girl said stubbornly to herself, *I may be sitting down on the outside, but I'm standing up on the inside.*

Ever been there? I sure have.

Whether Esther always agreed with Mordecai or not, she most likely realized that she had benefited from the blessings of obedience in the past, so she honored his advice in this instance as well. Esther trusted her cousin in this crucial moment because she respected the wisdom that had come with his age and his position as her "father." His dedication to her was evident, and she knew that he had her best interest at heart.

Esther had the same attitude of obedience when she came under the supervision of Hegai. She could have been haughty and thought that she didn't need the advice of some old guy. After all, she was already beautiful.

During Esther's twelve months of preparation, Hegai looked upon her with favor and gave her special care. Esther was mindful of his favor and came to trust that he, like Mordecai, was concerned with her well-being. As the king's servant, Hegai knew just what would touch the heart of the king. . .and it did. At the critical moment before she was to go before the king—the moment that would forever seal her fate—she maintained her teachable spirit and was willing to heed the advice of her supervisor. When Esther came before the king, she was cloaked with this same attitude of respect and obedience that she had shown Mordecai and Hegai, and again she received the blessing of obedience—favor.

God takes this issue of honor and respect so seriously that He gives a special promise to those who keep this commandment: "And this is the promise: If you honor your father and mother, 'you will live a long life, full of blessing'" (Ephesians 6:3, NLT). Again and again we see this promise from the Ten Commandments at work in Esther's life. You can bet that she received favor not merely because of physical beauty or feminine charm, but because she had a beautiful attitude of honor and obedience.

That's not true of many young people today. We live in a culture that celebrates rebellion and ridicules authority. Bumper stickers tell you to "Question Authority." The MTV generation thumbs their noses at their parents' values. Their role models are athletes and rock stars who don't respect authority. Yet even people who are deeply immersed in this culture still recognize the genuine beauty of a thoughtful, pleasant, and courteous person—as opposed to the ugliness of rebellion and disrespect.

EVERYBODY HAS TO OBEY SOMEBODY

Throughout your lifetime, you will have to submit to people and situations.

I remember trying to explain this to my three young daughters. One night after I had to punish them for disobeying, they cried out, "That's not *fair!*" I told them that God had given me the responsibility to help them learn to obey through self-control. If I didn't follow through with that, then God would hold me (their mommy) responsible—and I would have to answer to Him someday.

That was a new concept for them! Their little faces looked puzzled as they digested this thought. I went on to explain that *everybody* has to submit to *somebody*. I could see that, as much as they were able to comprehend it, the reality of a lifetime of submission was setting in. I could almost see the wheels turning in their minds as they thought, *Doesn't submission stop when you become a grown-up? Surely this can't be true!*

Finally one of them asked, "Mommy, who do *you* have to submit to?"

I replied that I have to obey the laws of the land that help keep us safe. I have to submit to my boss at work. As a Christian woman, I honor my husband as the spiritual leader of our home. And most of all, I have to obey God.

My oldest daughter began catching on to this chain of command idea. "Who does *Daddy* have to obey?" she asked.

You could see that they were realizing that this obedience thing is much more far-reaching than they had ever imagined. It extends far beyond the boundaries of their own home. When I explained that even

Daddy had to obey, there was silence…. They pondered this thought for quite some time. It finally took root: Even their daddy has to honor his boss, whether he agrees or not; obey God; and, yes, even receive discipline from God if necessary. Understanding that helped them to overcome the pain of injustice they had felt moments earlier.

How I wish I'd learned this principle earlier in life! This is not just about honor and respect for parents or for those in a position of authority in your life. The truth is that if you cannot apply this commandment to your life in a practical way, you will struggle to obey and submit to your heavenly Father, too. And that is a very serious matter.

If you get nothing else out of this chapter, **get this:**

 You cannot obey and submit to your heavenly Father if you have not learned to listen to and obey earthly authority. Your ability to be obedient in horizontal relationships with man is directly related to your ability to be obedient in a vertical relationship with God.

And if you don't learn how to hear and obey your heavenly Father, sooner or later you will find yourself walking straight into His discipline.

Please trust me in this. You don't want to go there!

God's time-outs are much more heart-wrenching than any punishment or disciplinary action you will ever receive in your home or at work. Scripture says, "Do not make light of the Lord's discipline, and do not lose heart when he rebukes you, because the Lord disciplines those he loves" (Hebrews 12:5–6).

THE BLESSINGS OF OBEDIENCE

Esther's attitude of honor and obedience gave her great influence at a very crucial moment in her life. That's another one of the blessings of obedience. As I've said, we don't know how many years passed between the time Esther became queen and the time she went before the king on behalf of her people. But if she had not displayed a submissive, respectful heart and attitude in her marriage, her husband might never have extended his scepter, opened his heart and mind, and given her the opportunity to make her plea. If she had not honored the king throughout their relationship, she might never have been in a position to intercede for her people at that critical moment.

An even greater example of obedience leading to blessing is that of our Lord Jesus. When He submitted Himself in obedience to baptism, *all heaven opened up!* The Holy Spirit rested on Him in the form of a dove, and God the Father declared in a voice that shook the ground, "This is my Son…with whom I am well pleased" (Matthew 3:17, emphasis mine).

And in the ultimate test of obedience, Jesus "humbled himself and became obedient to death—even death on a cross! Therefore God exalted him to the highest place and gave him the name that is above every name, that at the name of Jesus every knee should bow, in heaven and on earth and under the earth, and every tongue confess that Jesus Christ is Lord, to the glory of God the Father" (Philippians 2:8–11).

Incredible! Now that's favor! Clearly, as God has promised, blessing follows obedience. And as with Esther, the obedience of Jesus was not a one-time event, but a pattern—an attitude of obedience. And just as Esther's obedience led to salvation for her people, the obedience of Jesus produced eternal salvation for you and me.

RISE UP!

When Esther finally entered the king's chambers, she was wearing something more than expensive royal garments. She was robed with a sincere attitude of respect and obedience. It clothed her with a beauty beyond anything the king had ever seen—and he had seen quite a bit!

As a result, she received the blessing of the king's favor and was promoted to her new position as queen. Talk about a blessing!

Do you see the pattern here? Obedience and an attitude of honor lead to the blessing of favor, promotion, and position. This pattern applies to this life and to life in the kingdom of God as well. As a young woman of destiny, do you want the blessing of God's favor, promotion, and position so that you can affect this world for the kingdom? It all starts with an attitude of obedience...*for such a time as this.*

SEE IT, SAY IT, WALK IT OUT

- "And this is love: that we walk in obedience to his commands. As you have heard from the beginning, his command is that you walk in love." (2 John 1:6)
- "Does the LORD delight in burnt offerings and sacrifices as much as in obeying the voice of the LORD? To obey is better than sacrifice, and to heed is better than the fat of rams." (1 Samuel 15: 22)
- "We have all had human fathers who disciplined us and we respected them for it. How much more should we submit to the Father of our spirits and live!" (Hebrews 12:9)

JUST DO IT!

1. Ask the Lord to give you a divine appointment with obedience this week. When the situation arises, you'll know it's an Esther moment. It may involve a superior, or it may be God Himself asking you to step out and do something. Do it—and expect a blessing. It's a promise!

2. Journal It:
   What was your response, your thoughts and feelings, surrounding

the point of obedience. How did you do? What character was required?

_____

_____

_____

_____

_____

_____

_____

_____

_____

_____

_____

_____

_____

_____

_____

_____

 Get Real!

...forsuchatimeasthis

*Each young woman went to the king,
and she was given whatever she desired to take with her
from the women's quarters....
She [Esther] requested nothing but what Hegai...advised.*

ESTHER 2:13, 15, NKJV

B y the time it was Esther's turn to appear before the king in the royal reviewing room, he must have thought he'd seen it all.

Women by the dozen—a seemingly endless parade of hopeful beauty contestants.

Every dolled-up dancer.

Every dewy-eyed ingenue.

Every sultry, scarf-clad songbird flaunting her feminine charms.

He'd seen all the moves, all the fluttering eyelashes, all the subtle gestures, all the seductive little pouts. The whole nine yards. He'd witnessed every choreographed entrance, every feverish audition, every frantic tap dance. Bleary-eyed, his staff had pored over every résumé and eight-by-ten-inch glossy. If the slaves hadn't worked overtime fanning the air, they all would have choked on the perfume that filled the royal chambers. The king of the Persian Empire met countless young women that had lost sight of who they were in a desperate attempt to be who they thought he wanted them to be.

Then came Esther.

No props. No pretense. No memorized lines. No glitter. No flash. No sequins. No slinky Hollywood moves. Nothing to compel or demand the king's attention. Just Esther, offering nothing but herself. She took no bribes to get special placement; she brought no schemes to manipulate the king's favor. She was real, vulnerable, transparent.

The contrast must have been a breath of fresh air.

THE BIG MOMENT

What might Esther have been thinking about as she readied herself to appear before the king? How could she help but size up all the glamorous women milling around her, wondering how she compared? (You know how we can be!) These were the most gorgeous women in the empire—dazzling beauties clad in all the latest knockout styles.

It was enough to make an orphaned Jewish girl feel a little unsure of herself, don't you think? A little insecure, maybe? Esther might have battled the temptation of adorning herself with some combination of baubles and bangles and gold-threaded garments to help her stand out from the crowd. She might have asked for some kind of security blanket to take into the king's chambers. You know, like a lucky rabbit's foot or something.

But when she had the opportunity to claim something—anything—from the ornate women's wing of the palace, Esther asked for nothing more than what Hegai suggested to her. She trusted his judgment. Whatever else he might have recommended, I can imagine Hegai, who had taken a liking to her from the beginning, giving Esther that age-old advice: "Just be yourself."

In the midst of an insecure situation, Esther remained who she was and resisted the temptation to mask her true self. When the king first set eyes on her, he didn't have to guess who she was behind some elaborate costume or silky veil. He could see exactly who she was.

When you stop to think about it, this is what the Lord desires from us, too. He wants us to come to Him unmasked. He knows exactly who and what we are, and He desires honesty at the deepest level. David said it well in Psalm 51:6: "Surely you desire truth in the inner parts; you teach me wisdom in the inmost place." David realized that God wanted no pretense, no phoniness, no religious glaze painted over a cold, insincere heart. It was no different in Esther's day...or in ours. God values an open, honest heart.

WILL THE REAL YOU PLEASE STAND UP?

I once read a story about Michelangelo in which the famous sculptor and painter was hauling a heavy stone up a hill. When someone called out to him and asked why he was dragging the huge stone, the artist replied, "Because there is an angel in there that wants to come out."

That's a beautiful picture of how God wants to chisel away all the unnecessary outer "stuff" to turn us into what He created us to be—a person made in His image. Of course there wasn't *really* an angel inside that lump of stone—but Michelangelo looked at it and saw something more. He saw what it could be. In just the same way, God looks at our fallen nature, our sinful hearts, and sees the potential for something more.

God knows how to bring out His image in you if you will lay aside your insecurities and masquerades and allow Him to make you into a woman after His own heart. Listen to what the apostle Paul said: "And we, who with unveiled faces all reflect the Lord's glory, are being trans-formed into his likeness with ever-increasing glory, which comes from the Lord, who is the Spirit" (2 Corinthians 3:18).

As we begin to look more and more like Jesus, there is no need to hide behind anything. We can be real. We can be secure in the knowledge that God is chipping away at us, transforming us into a person who, like Esther, can stand before the King without fear. We can be content with who God made us to be.

AN ESTHER MOMENT

From the journal of a modern-day Esther:

Strength is her canvas
with shades of vulnerability
and compassion.
how she longs for the
Artist
to finish her portrait.

Quite
uncommon
to discover
a mirror to
my soul
in
you.

—Lisa Dauffenbauch[5]

PROPS, COSTUMES, AND THE MAKEUP DEPARTMENT

What is the mask you hide behind? Your looks? Your talents, education, or success? Trust me, there will always be someone skinnier, more beautiful, more talented, smarter, and more successful than you. Do you feel that you have to spend money on clothes, cars, or going to all the latest cool places with all the latest cool people who have all the latest cool stuff just to feel like you're "somebody"? I've tried it, but I've discovered that no amount of success or excitement can fill the emptiness inside if you can't be content with who you are and with what you have.

In a letter from his prison cell, Paul told the church at Philippi:

For I have learned to be content whatever the circumstances. I know what it is to be in need, and I know what it is to have plenty. I have learned the secret of being content in any and every situation, whether well fed or hungry, whether living in plenty or in want. I can do everything through him who gives me strength. (Philippians 4:11–13)

Are you content with your situation? Or do you feel insecure if you don't have lots of dates or a new boyfriend to cling to? Before I was married, I made *that* mistake, too—using boyfriends as a crutch for my nagging insecurities. Some girls aren't even aware of when they go into flirt mode, needing attention from the opposite sex just to feel desirable and worthy of notice. If you don't know who you are, you will become a chameleon, easily persuaded to take on the identity of each new guy that comes into your life.

Remember the movie *Runaway Bride*? Julia Roberts's character kept running from the altar and from commitment. With each new relationship, she took on the identity of the man in her life. In the end (with a little help from Richard Gere), she realized that she didn't know who *she* was. She didn't even know how she liked her eggs cooked. She knew how to become whatever some guy wanted her to be, but she didn't know how to be herself.

All these things are veils and masks we hide behind in an effort to convince people that we're something we're not so that they will love and accept us. And do you know what? That's exactly where Satan, the enemy of our soul, wants to keep us—bound and living a lie.

GET REAL WITH YOUR BAD SELF

Perhaps there was a negative experience in your past that hurt you emotionally or made you feel insecure. As a coping method, we often put up walls of anger, resentment, or false confidence to protect ourselves from being hurt again.

Or perhaps you hide behind the person you want others to see. How often we feel that need to strive for perfection in school, sports, career, physical attractiveness, or accomplishments in order to be liked and accepted by others. But that, too, is a false projection of who we really are.

I can remember the awful hurts in my life that made me want to hide my wounds, to project some kind of image that would make people like and admire me. I couldn't let them see the real Lisa:

...insecure over my parents' divorce,
...brokenhearted and lost after my brother's death,
...out of control, compulsive, and suffering from an eating disorder,
...searching for security and acceptance through boyfriends,
...suppressing and denying the anger that burned inside.

I felt like such a mess inside that I needed to masquerade as Miss Perfection, the girl who had it all together. I kept trying to "find myself" when the truth was that I needed to find out who God had created me to be.

Only He could uncover and heal my pain. Only He could show me who I really was. Only He could forgive my sins, my rebellion, and shed light on all the dark places in my heart, making me clean and pure within. I wasn't even aware that I constantly caught a glimpse of myself in every mirror I passed, only to take quick inventory of how I measured up and to check out the facade I hid behind. God was the only mirror I needed. And the more I gazed at Him in His Word, the more I began to see and understand who I really was.

What I first saw when the Holy Spirit shone His bright light into the corners of my heart wasn't very pretty. In fact, there was a lot of ugliness inside. I was shocked at what I saw: anger, unforgivingness, selfish ambition, pride, and ego.

God wasn't revealing these things to me in order to discourage me or rub my nose in them. He was showing me the way to forgiveness, peace, and self-acceptance. He was showing me how to live like a secure, content daughter of the King. That kind of transformation doesn't come by dwelling on our past and our failures. It comes from looking to the future. "I do not consider myself yet to have taken hold of it," Paul said, "but…I press on toward the goal to win the prize for which God has called me heavenward in Christ Jesus" (Philippians 3:13–14).

When a young woman comes to terms with who she is in Christ— her true identity in Him—*nothing* can stop her. She will no longer fear what others might think of her or say about her or how she "compares" with others. She will be confident, not in herself but in Christ. And that makes the kingdom of darkness tremble. It's time to expose the dark places in your heart to the light of God…and get real.

WHAT IS REAL?

Sometimes children's stories illustrate a point so beautifully. In the classic book *The Velveteen Rabbit,* a little stuffed rabbit—who is snubbed by some of the more expensive toys because he is stuffed with sawdust and has no moving parts—hears the other toys talking about being "real," and he wonders what that means. The oldest and wisest toy in the nursery, the Skin Horse, explains:

> "Real isn't how you are made," said the Skin Horse. "It's a thing that happens to you. When a child loves you for a long, long time, not just to play with, but *really* loves you, then you become Real."
>
> "Does it hurt?" asked the Rabbit.
>
> "Sometimes," said the Skin Horse, for he was always truthful. "When you are Real you don't mind being hurt."
>
> "Does it happen all at once, like being wound up," he asked, "or bit by bit?"
>
> "It doesn't happen all at once," said the Skin Horse. "You become. It takes a long time. That's why it doesn't often happen to people who break easily, or have sharp edges, or who have to be carefully kept. Generally, by the time you are Real, most of your hair has been loved off, and your eyes drop out and you get loose in the joints and very shabby. But these things don't matter at all, because once you are Real you can't be ugly, except to people who don't understand." [6]

For a more grown-up story about being real instead of hiding behind masks or veils, check out Till We Have Faces, by C. S. Lewis. Also worth reading is "The Minister's Black Veil," a short story by Nathaniel Hawthorne.

Esther was real. And just like the Skin Horse said, it didn't happen overnight. It was a process, a lifetime of being real before God. Because she knew who she was as a child of God, she could be real in front of the king of Persia.

YOU'RE INVITED TO A "COME AS YOU ARE" PARTY

The thing I love about this part of Esther's story is that it demonstrates how we are to come into the presence of *our* King. What freedom there is in knowing that I can come before my King—even with my insecurities, failures, and disappointments—and that He will receive me and accept me just as I am. I don't have to pretend in front of Him. In fact, if anyone is going to see through an act, it's God. There's no way I could ever fool Him. I can come to Him at any time, and He will hold out His scepter and look upon His child with love, acceptance, and favor.

RISE UP!

Do you know God in this way? Do you have the confidence to stand before Him—and others—completely unafraid because you know you are His daughter? If you don't, then pray this prayer:

Heavenly Father, I come before You just as I am. Lord, the sin in my life has caused me to hide from You. I ask You to forgive me for the things I have done that disappoint You. Today, I let down my guard and acknowledge the pain and insecurity that You already see so well. Lord, I give it to You now and ask You to heal the wounded places. God, help me to see myself as You see me. Reveal to me the veils I am hiding behind and the false security I am leaning on instead of You. Help me to leave them at the threshold of Your chamber as I come into Your presence. Take me and love me as I am. Help me to walk honestly and openly before others as I am now before You.

As long as you hide behind your veil of insecurity and mask who you really are, you cannot fulfill your destiny. Let's get real, *for such a time as this.*

SEE IT, SAY IT, WALK IT OUT

- "Now we see but a poor reflection as in a mirror; then we shall see face to face. Now I know in part; then I shall know fully, even as I am fully known." (1 Corinthians 13:12)
- "LORD, you have searched me and you know me. You know when I sit and when I rise; you perceive my thoughts from afar. You discern my going out and my lying down; you are familiar with all my ways. Before a word is on my tongue you know it completely, O LORD." (Psalm 139:1–4)
- "Nothing in all creation is hidden from God's sight. Everything is uncovered and laid bare before the eyes of him to whom we must give account." (Hebrews 4:13)

JUST DO IT!

1. Time to do a little spring-cleaning! List things that you have put your identity in other than Christ (i.e., looks, achievements, popularity, boyfriends), and ask God to help you let go of false reality.

   _____

   _____

   _____

   _____

   _____

   _____

   _____

2. 📓 Journal It:

    Write down how you see yourself. Then ask a trusted friend to tell you how she sees you. If there are major differences, you need to take a hard look at those areas to see if you're hiding behind a veil that needs to be torn away.

    _____

    _____

    _____

    _____

    _____

    _____

    _____

    _____

    _____

    _____

    _____

    _____

    _____

Finding Favor

...forsuchatimeasthis

Esther won the favor of everyone who saw her.

ESTHER 2:15

D id Esther receive favor just because of her beauty? Was it because the rest of the harem had voted her "most likely to succeed"? Did she become queen as the result of a popularity contest, kind of like being crowned homecoming queen or Miss Congeniality? It's often tempting to link popularity and attention with favor, but trust me, any relationship between the two is quite often purely coincidental!

Think about the popular girls from your high school or college. Maybe you have been one of them. They seemed to have it all—looks, boyfriends, friends, great clothes—but did those things last? Anyone who's been to a high school or college reunion knows that the popular people aren't necessarily those who succeed—who gain "favor"—in spite of having been top dogs in school.

Certainly Esther must have been aware of the extra attention she was getting. But how often have you seen a pretty girl who gets a lot of attention let it go to her head and act really ugly? Do people really want to be around her other than to use her attractiveness for their own benefit?

Esther was nothing like that. The truly beautiful thing about her is that her physical beauty was only part of who she was—it didn't define her. God knew the condition of her heart, and He knew that He could trust her with His favor. God gave her favor so that He could place her in the right place at the right time. It was not granted to an undeserving, selfish, conceited brat, and like all godly favor, it was undeserved. It's not about looks, wealth, or popularity. It's God's hand resting on you—and it's always for a reason that's bigger than you are.

 Remember this; it's important. Take out your pen and underline it. If God's favor is resting on you, it's not about you, just like it wasn't about Esther. God does not grant His favor just for the good of one person. It's always because He wants to use that one person to advance His Kingdom. But favor also comes with a responsibility. As Mordecai reminded Esther, if you're not willing or able to be used, He'll find someone else who is.

Beauty, talent, and intelligence may get you worldly attention, but that favor is fleeting compared to the favor that rests on a child of God, obedient in heart and humble in spirit.

DIG A LITTLE DEEPER

The word *favor* is used seven times in the book of Esther. That makes it a major theme. So let's take a look at the word favor and dig a little deeper.

Because the English language is limited, we sometimes miss the true meaning of words. According to Webster's Dictionary, the word favor means "friendly regard toward another, especially by a superior; approving consideration or attention."

That makes sense, doesn't it? Hegai and the king both have friendly regard toward Esther, so they give her approving consideration or attention. But there's a reason why your pastor always talks about the "original Hebrew" of a word—because although we may translate the word as favor, which is the best English fit, it's not exactly what the original Hebrew word meant. I know this may sound like you're back in class, but before you zone out, just look at what I found.

Read the word favor in context in the book of Esther. You'll find it in Esther 2:9, 15, 17; 5:2, 8; 7:3; 8:5.

FAVOR WITH A PURPOSE

In this case, favor refers to unmerited favor from a divine source with a far greater purpose than mere approval by man as a result of charm or beauty. Though Esther is both charming and beautiful, that's not why or how she receives favor.

In two very significant instances (Esther 2:9, when Esther receives favor from Hegai, and Esther 2:17, when she receives favor from Xerxes), the actual Hebrew word for favor is *chesed* or *hesed.* This is a covenant word that's not used in a secular context, as we understand favor. Hesed is a uniquely Jewish, Old Testament term used to denote Jehovah God's covenant-keeping power.

In other words, although we read that Esther found favor in the eyes of Hegai, the supervisor of the women, and Xerxes, the king, it was really God's favor that was on her. God rests His favor on those He intends to use to carry out His plan.

Although the author of Esther does not overtly express God's leading in the book, it is clearly implied in the use of this word, which is unique to the relationship between the covenant God, Jehovah, and His chosen people, the Jews. His favor rested on them simply because He had chosen them, not because they deserved it in any way. We, too, through Christ, have become God's chosen people—a royal priesthood, a holy nation (1 Peter 2:9)—and we, too, benefit from God's covenant-keeping power, hesed.

So you can see that this favor is much more than just attention paid to a pretty girl. There were hundreds, maybe thousands, of beautiful women for the King to choose from, but God's favor rested only on Esther. Covenant favor! Esther is God's hesed for the entire nation of Israel. He is keeping covenant with them through her. In a very real sense, she is like the parted waters and dry land that provided the Jews a way of escape from Pharaoh. That favor was given to her for a specific purpose. And if you are a child of God, His hesed rests on you.

Divine favor is a distinguishing mark of God's presence on his people and is always for a greater purpose. Read about these fellow friends in favor:

• Joseph found favor (Genesis 39).
• Daniel was shown favor (Daniel 1 & 2).
• Mary was highly favored (Luke 1:28, 30).

This revelation is very liberating. It frees us from having to perform. It frees us from the weight of feeling that we have to fulfill our destiny on our own. Of course, we have a responsibility to be obedient to God's Word and walk in godly character, but His covenant-keeping power is at work on our behalf.

God's favor, presence, and blessing carry us through the inevitable crises in life. Divine favor always leads to greater position and responsibility as we walk out our destiny. It's always about something bigger than us. And the key is obedience.

I work with Gordon Robertson, Pat Robertson's son. When asked what was the most important piece of advice his father gave him growing up, he said, "Be bless-able." Be bless-able. God wants to bless us and have his favor rest upon us for the purpose of His work in the Kingdom and because He is a good Father who desires to give good things to His children.

Esther experienced great blessing and favor because of the way she lived her life. She was pure, submissive, courageous, humble, and full of grace, which put her in a position to be bless-able. She was obedient in character. As a result, God knew He could trust her with the favor to be His hesed for the Jewish people. These were choices that she made, and you can, too. Choose to be bless-able. Live a life of obedience, and experience God's favor at work in your life.

AN *E*STHER MOMENT

To show you what I mean, let me tell you about my own experience with God's favor and how I came to be a cohost on *The 700 Club*. I am humbled when I think back on everything God has done on my behalf over the last few years.

I realize now that it all started several years ago: God was calling me to obedience. He was making it clear that I needed to lay down my aspirations for a career in television. I was just beginning to get some decent work, but my dream had become an idol and much of my self-worth was wrapped up in it. It was a slow and painful death, but eventually I released it to God. I put that dream on the shelf and vowed never to pick it up again unless God opened the door.

Years before, while watching *The 700 Club*, I had told God that I would love to work for that ministry someday. I was impressed by their professionalism and obvious passion for God. At the time I had said, "God, I'll do anything just to be a part of that great ministry." Be careful what you pray for!

Little did I know that God was orchestrating events even then to bring us to Virginia Beach. With me eight months pregnant and our two young daughters in tow, our family took a step of obedience and moved across the country so that my husband, Marcus, could pursue a graduate degree at Regent University. We left family, friends, and security to follow God's leading.

Several years earlier I had been on *The 700 Club* to give my testimony when I was Miss California, which led to some work for CBN. I knew several people there, but I had let go of that whole TV thing and wasn't about to get on the phone and say, "Look, here I am—remember me?" I was fully content to be a full-time mommy. We were here so my husband could get his degree, and when he was done, we would be on the next plane back to California, our home.

Then one day my husband noticed a job posting that I was qualified for. It was in the Operations Department at CBN. The operations crew is the technical, behind-the-scenes team that makes *The 700 Club* happen—camera people, audio technicians, director, teleprompter operator, etc. I didn't really want to go back to work, especially with a newborn at home. But we needed the money, and it wouldn't be forever. I applied for the job and got it.

Marcus tackled the role of Mr. Mom by day and took classes and studied at night. For almost a year I wore jeans, work boots, and a ponytail to work and was "one of the guys." On breaks I would sneak to the restroom with a breast pump so I could continue nursing. Madelin was just eight weeks old when I started. That was a very hard year, but we were thankful for God's provision.

Then came a chain of events that changed my life. As Pat Robertson likes to say, he "discovered" me.

One day in the studio, after taping *The 700 Club,* Pat called everyone back to look at some lighting and camera angles. He was directing the meeting and asked me to stand in for Terry. Talk about being ready when the King calls! I'm not sure if Pat remembered me at the time, but I had met him years earlier, so I was comfortable talking with him as we walked through some of the elements of the show. It was a little strange to be in front of the camera again, but I was just a "stand-in" and happy to oblige. Afterward, others commented that Pat was very at ease with me and that I had favor with him.

Then things began to move with astonishing swiftness.

One day I was called into the office of one of the vice presidents. Afraid of what I'd done to be summoned by one of the higher-ups, I could feel my heart pounding as I entered the office and faced the VP. "Are you the same Lisa Ryan, Lisa Davenport Ryan [my maiden name], that was Miss California and guest-hosted *The 700 Club* several years ago?" he asked.

"Yes, sir," I said.

"Thank you," he said, smiling.

End of interview.

I now know that God was working behind the scenes.

A few days later I was called into another meeting with the executive producer of *The 700 Club*. He, too, inquired about my background and asked why I hadn't mentioned my on-camera experience on my résumé. I explained that I wasn't applying for an on-camera position and thought it might hinder me from getting the job I had applied for.

He then asked me if I had any résumé tape and if I was willing to do a camera test. This was something I had laid down at the feet of God many years before! If that dead dream was going to come off the shelf, I wanted to be sure it was God, not me. I was afraid even to let myself think, *What if?* Almost reluctantly, I made a tape and turned it in.

A few weeks went by and nothing. Then, as I was filling in in the wardrobe department one day, I got a call and was asked if I could do a camera test the next day.

Let me put this in perspective for you. That *never* happens. No one goes from running teleprompter and laundering Pat's shirts to working on camera. That's like Cinderella going to the ball—impossible. What were they thinking? I hadn't worked in front of the camera for years. Besides that, I still had some weight on from the baby and didn't even have an appropriate TV outfit. That night Marcus, the kids, and I went out and "blew our wad" on an attractive suit. Then we called everyone back home and asked them to pray…for favor.

I was a wreck the next day as I started to make the transformation from crew gal to Katie Couric. It had been a long time since I had done TV hair and makeup. It was a surreal feeling, walking into the studio that day. I regularly turned words on the teleprompter, but it had been a long time since I had had to read them while sounding natural and looking perky. The crew gave me a bad time, but I was comforted to be among friends. I breathed a big sigh, and away we went with the audition.

Soon I was called to yet another meeting where I was told that they needed someone to fill in for Terry Meeuwsen on occasion. Without a backup person, she couldn't take a sick day or personal time off. I greatly admired Terry and was honored to help out where I could. I found out later that Terry had suggested they give me a chance, and I am still thankful for her support.

I was also asked to be a feature producer the rest of the time. God was taking that old dream off the shelf. It was frightening and exhilarating all at once.

But it wasn't all smooth sailing. I was never more keenly aware of God's favor than in those first days and weeks that I covered for Terry. Jumping back on that bike wasn't as easy as I thought it would be. I made some on-camera faux pas that are painful to think about even today. Every day I was sure that I was going to get "the phone call" saying, "Thank you for playing…. Next!"

Amazingly, by the grace of God, Pat and others encouraged me. People continued to point out that I had found favor. That favor made me keenly aware that this wasn't about me. Now, five years later and as a full-time cohost on *The 700 Club,* I am always mindful that it is only God's divine favor that has positioned me to speak to thousands of people every day and tell them about the incredible redeeming love of God.

Rise Up!

As a princess in God's court, you have His favor, His hesed upon you. He is always at work, not only keeping His end of the covenant, but helping you keep yours, too. Listen quietly to His still small voice saying, "This is the way, walk in it." Be at peace and *rest* in God's favor. When He calls you, *stand* in His favor. And when He sounds the charge, *walk* confidently and boldly in favor *for such a time as this.*

See It, Say It, Walk It Out

- "Never let loyalty and kindness get away from you! Wear them like a necklace; write them deep within your heart. Then you will find favor with both God and people, and you will gain a good reputation." (Proverbs 3:3–4, NLT)
- "And so God can always point to us as examples of the incredible wealth of his favor and kindness toward us, as shown in all he has done for us through Christ Jesus." (Ephesians 2:7, NLT)
- "Then everyone will give honor to the name of our Lord Jesus because of you, and you will be honored along with him. This is all made possible because of the undeserved favor of our God and Lord, Jesus Christ." (2 Thessalonians 1:12, NLT)

Just Do It!

1. Over the next week or so, take time to observe people. Look at them with spiritual eyes, and see if you spot someone with

"favor" upon her. This may sound crazy, but try it. When someone has "Esther favor" on her, you will be able to spot it.

2. If you want to have God's redemptive favor upon you, remember that it's not about you; it's about God's purpose. Then pray this very simple prayer:

WARNING:

This is one of those dangerous kinds of prayers that could change your life, so make sure you're ready.

Lord, I ask that You would grant me favor in Your sight and in the sight of man, that through my life You would further Your kingdom and purposes in heaven and on earth. Amen.

chapter nine

In Position for Promotion

...forsuchatimeasthis

And the king loved Esther more than all the women, and she found favor and kindness with him more than all the virgins, so that he set the royal crown on her head and made her queen instead of Vashti.

ESTHER 2:17, NASB

AND THE WINNER IS...

And the winner of a life of lavish royalty in the palace, a brand-new sports chariot, a custom designed haute-couture wardrobe, and a lifetime supply of oil of myrrh…the new first lady of the greatest kingdom in the world, the Queen of Persia is—the envelope, please—*Esther*!"

The crowd roars; the music swells—then the crown, the robe, the sash, the flowers, the runway walk, and Burt Parks singing, "There she is, Miss Persia; there she is, our ideal!"

Okay, so maybe it wasn't quite like that. But still, Esther had won the king's favor and been promoted to her new position as queen of an empire so vast that it spread from India and western China up into the southern part of the former Soviet Union, the Middle East, Egypt, and into Ethiopia. Get out a map and look at it. It was quite a kingdom, and Esther reigned over all of it. Wow—and all by the age of twenty or so! That's quite a position of responsibility.

It Doesn't "Just Happen"

Esther was living out her destiny. She had risen to the coveted position of queen. But it didn't just happen overnight. Preparation for her position of royalty had begun during her childhood. She had survived losing her parents—a tragedy that brought her under Mordecai's care. From him she learned obedience, which helped her submit to the good advice of Hegai. In turn, Hegai's favor and special care helped Esther's physical beauty to be at its peak when she went before the king.

Years of faithful dedication had positioned Esther to achieve her destiny when the time came. She understood who she was, and despite all the pressures during the twelve months of preparation, she remained true to herself and transparent and honest before others. Favor placed her in a position to be promoted. All that had gone before was preparation for such a time as this. I'm sure that each girl there thought that becoming queen would be the pinnacle of her destiny— that she would have "arrived." But for Esther, who walked in the disciplines of destiny that we've talked about, becoming queen must have been somewhat baffling. What purpose could there possibly be in being the trophy wife of a vain king?

In reality, Esther's position was just a means to an end. She was merely being put in the right place at the right time. From this position she would be able to speak the truth that would save her people.

When we look back over the course of our lives, we can see how past events have shaped our present situations. For example, for years I felt drawn to be part of a ministry that combined my interest in television with an eternal purpose of transforming people's lives. My time as Miss California prepared me and opened doors in the television and broadcasting industry. Those positions in turn gave me the experience that I now draw from every day on *The 700 Club*, a position that has given me a platform for this new position as an author, from which I can minister specifically to young women.

Don't misunderstand. I'm not suggesting that life is one mountain-top experience after another. Believe me, there have been plenty of low valleys that have helped shape and prepare me as well. In addition to some painful trials in childhood, there was a very difficult season early in our marriage when Marcus and I lost everything financially. That crisis put our vows to the test: We had to come together to fight for our marriage. We grew together and with the Lord, which helped me to develop the godly character and maturity essential to the position I now hold.

Really difficult times often lead to a God-given position. There were plenty of times when I didn't see how God could ever bring me from that desolate place and fulfill the dreams He had placed in my heart, but He did. Most of the time we don't see the big picture. Too often, we see each step along the way to our ultimate destiny as an end in itself—or, in some cases, as the end of our world. In reality, each new situation is for our preparation and is a piece of the destiny puzzle. Even the difficult times are "training for reigning." With each new position, our destiny and vision come into greater focus, and we begin to get the big picture.

An *Esther* Moment

Several months ago, I began noticing the same girl every Sunday sitting in the front row at church by herself. Week after week, there she was. She was always dressed fashionably yet modestly with her hair neatly styled. I couldn't help but notice how she participated in worship, clapping and singing. I didn't see any parents or friends sitting with her. She participated fully in the service all by herself. When it came time for the message, she opened her Bible and attentively took notes. Why was this pretty girl always sitting alone?

After a few months, I noticed a couple more kids joining her up front. Shortly after that there were a handful of young people actively participating in the service. She had assumed a set apart position, and others had followed.

Then one Sunday, as I was picking up my girls after a later service, I saw this same young lady assisting in children's church. I asked the children's coordinator about her, and she spoke highly of this girl, commenting on how good she was with kids and that she had appointed her to help teach the younger children. I was also surprised to find out that this young lady had even resigned from a coveted position on a competitive gymnastics team because she was bothered by the conduct of her teammates. If you can believe it, she also cut her beautiful long hair and donated it to be made into a wig for a cancer patient.

I consistently observed character in this young lady that caught my attention, and I couldn't help but think that she was like a young Esther.

Some time had gone by when I saw her again at an after-school function, this time with a friend and a woman who appeared to be her mother. By now I was so curious that I had to find out her name and what it was that made her so special. I introduced myself to her and her mom. I explained that I had been watching her for some time, which I'm sure sounded like some crazy church lady stalker, now that I think of it!

She politely told me that her name was Tori and that the reason she sat in the front row was so she wouldn't get distracted. She really liked the pastor's teaching and didn't want to miss anything. Her face lit up as she talked about how much she enjoyed working with the kids in children's church and some of the other ministry opportunities she was looking forward to. But do you want to know the truly amazing thing about this modern-day Esther named Tori?

She's twelve years old.

Yet she's already walking in the character that has positioned her among her peers, teachers, and leaders in the church. Tori is an excellent example of what I call a young Esther rising, and you can be one, too.

Stepping into Position

If you, like Esther, are living a life of purity and obedience, one marked by the inner beauty that comes from those qualities and a willingness to be set apart, then you are becoming a person that God can use. You will begin to sense the Lord's favor moving you into new and greater positions of responsibility. Each new position not only fulfills your destiny, but is also a part of God's greater purpose.

Your teachers, pastor, or boss may recognize the qualities of character we've talked about and ask you to consider taking a leadership position. A teacher may ask you to tutor another student struggling with a subject, or the pastor may ask you to consider teaching a Sunday school class. If you are responsible in your job, you may get a raise or promotion. You may assume a position of leadership among your peers without even realizing it.

Although your own position might not seem like much to you, the fact is that we all hold some kind of position. And it's our response to the position we're in that determines whether we're able to take on more responsibility. Tori's desire to please God in worship led her to assume a role of leadership among her peers. In my own experience, I have seen that there are three ways we can respond to the promotion of position that favor brings.

Passively

Esther could have been understandably insecure about moving into her new position as queen. Vashti was very beautiful, and Esther could easily have begun to compare herself with her predecessor. Esther had definitely married into money and out of her social comfort zone. That can be a very insecure position to be in. What would people's expectations of her be in the shadow of the bold and beautiful Vashti? Esther could easily have responded to her new position out of fear or self-conscious insecurity, but she didn't. She remained confident but humble, content in who she was, just as she had been when she came before the king.

Too often we as females compare ourselves with other females. This weakens our position by causing us to respond out of insecurity. When we do this, we are no longer being true to ourselves: We're responding out of our flesh, not in the Spirit.

I remember when I was first asked to fill in for Terry Meeuwsen as guest-host on *The 700 Club*. I had experience in television, but it had been several years since I had done any acting or broadcasting. This had been a desire of my heart for years. Yet when the opportunity came, everything in me wanted to retreat and convince God that he had the wrong girl. I had tremendous respect for Terry, both as a woman of God and as a professional. For years I had admired her sincerity and ease on camera. How could I ever match up to the standard of grace and ability she had demonstrated?

It took several months before I became comfortable enough to relax and be myself in the position God was moving me into. I had to stop trying to be Terry and be myself. That was an insecure time! But I'm stronger for having faced my fear and not retreating. When God gets you in position, He doesn't want you to react passively. His favor got you there, and it will keep you there until He has somewhere else He wants you to be.

Pridefully

Another response to position is one of pride, when you start to think, *It's all about me.* Oh, sure, in the beginning you knew that God had you where you were for a reason. But then you start to think, *Yeah, but I wouldn't have gotten here if I weren't so* _____ (smart, pretty, talented, witty—you fill in the blank). Once that kind of thinking seeps in, it's not so hard to think that you can rely on your own abilities to make the next move.

Remember Vashti? She obviously had a lot of confidence in herself to deny the king's request to come to him (Esther 1:12). As a result of her action, the king divorced her, stripped her of her position, and banished her. She was lucky to be alive! Perhaps her pride led her to deny the king's request. She may have thought that her position was so secure that even her refusal would not have serious consequences. Whatever the reason, her position was secure only as long as God allowed it to be. Her downfall was part of God's providential plan to put Esther on the throne in her place.

Sometimes, God needs a certain kind of person to fill a role for a certain time.

In Esther's case, he needed a beautiful young woman who would catch the eye of the king and who had a heart for God. Esther fit the bill. But as we've seen, it wasn't *just* that she was beautiful. There were qualities about her that made her pleasing—qualities that would have been lost if she had let pride puff her up.

Responsibly

Many years ago, when I first got an inkling that I was being called to CBN but before I ever came to work for *The 700 Club*, I read Pat Robertson's book *The Secret Kingdom*. It radically changed my perspective on the kingdom of God and my part in it. Pat lays out several kingdom principles that are at work in the lives of productive believers. One of them is taken from Luke 12:48: "To whom much is given, much is required." Pat calls this the Law of Responsibility.

The French phrase *noblesse oblige*—literally, *nobility obligates,* honorable behavior considered to be the responsibility of those of high birth—expresses the essence of the law of responsibility. Pat points out that people of rank, position, or favor are obligated to behave nobly, kindly, and responsibly toward others. Favor carries with it responsibility. As the favor increases, the responsibility increases. It's very wrong to ask God for something and not accept the responsibility that goes with it. Esther neither retreated from her position in insecurity nor flaunted it in pride. She acted responsibly in her new noble role as queen, and her acceptance of the obligation that came with position gave her the resolve and courage to face the coming crisis.

WEARING THE ROYAL ROBES

In the Bible, a person's outer robe, or mantle, represents his or her position of leadership or prominence. One modern-day example is a priest who wears a robe or collar to communicate his position of authority in the church. For instance, you don't have to see a close-up of the guy standing on the balcony at the Vatican in the flowing robes to know it's the Pope.

Esther 5:1 says: "On the third day Esther put on her royal robes and stood in the inner court of the palace, in front of the king's hall. The king was sitting on his royal throne in the hall, facing the entrance." Royal robe in place, Esther was ready to use her position for God's purpose.

Since this passage specifically tells us that Esther put on her royal robes, perhaps she wasn't in the habit of wearing them. The king probably sensed that she had something important on her mind to appear outside his throne room dressed as his queen.

Esther's royal robes represented her mantle of leadership as queen. By wearing them, she was not just getting gussied up to make an impression for a date. Her royal robes spoke of her position and gave her the confidence to go before the king with her request when it counted the most. Could this be what got his attention and made him extend his scepter to her?

As Christians, we also have royal robes that allow us to go before the throne room of God, royal apparel that He Himself has given us— the righteousness of Jesus! As a princess in God's court you have a position of royalty and are called to live your life by higher standards than the rest of the world. That position alone carries with it a great responsibility. You, like Esther, have an obligation of nobility.

Rise Up!

You may not see your particular big picture yet. But God's cosmic big picture is His kingdom: "Thy Kingdom come. Thy will be done in earth, as it is in heaven" (Matthew 6:10, KJV). As a princess in God's court, you can rise up with confidence in the royal robe that the King of kings has placed upon you. Walk and live in a manner worthy of your position, full of character and compassion. Through obedience you will receive favor on your journey of destiny. When you receive favor that leads to position, will you respond passively, pridefully, or responsibly? Noblesse oblige... *for such a time as this.*

See It, Say It, Walk It Out

- "For promotion and power come from nowhere on earth, but only from God. He promotes one and deposes another." (Psalm 75:6–7, TLB)
- "I urge you to live a life worthy of the calling you have received." (Ephesians 4:1)
- "His master replied, 'Well done, good and faithful servant! You have been faithful with a few things; I will put you in charge of many things. Come and share your master's happiness!'" (Matthew 25:21)

Just Do It!

1. List all the positions of responsibility in your life right now, from

the smallest to the greatest (i.e., student, employee, group leader, team member, teacher, family member...).

_____

_____

_____

_____

_____

_____

_____

_____

2. In some or all of these responsibilities you are being positioned for something to come, and how you handle these responsibilities will dramatically affect your future. List some of the responsibilities you would like to steward better. Beside each one, write out what you plan to do to responsibly walk in that position.

_____

_____

_____

_____

_____

_____

_____

_____

Crisis Happens

...forsuchatimeasthis

"Do not think in your heart that you will escape in the king's palace any more than all the other Jews. For if you remain completely silent at this time, relief and deliverance will arise for the Jews from another place, but you and your father's house will perish."

ESTHER 4:13–14, NKJV

Yes, the title of this chapter means exactly what you're thinking it means. Like the bumper sticker suggests, doo-doo happens.

On the threshold of a destiny she doesn't yet see, Esther faces the crisis of her life. How she responds will impact not only her own future, but also that of her family and people. This is the only time in the book of Esther that we see any indication of fear or hesitation on her part. And who wouldn't be afraid?

Here's the situation. Remember Haman from our cast of characters at the beginning of the book? The major racist? Well, in his burning hatred of Mordecai the Jew, Haman has managed to talk Esther's husband, the king, into signing an edict that will get rid of not only Mordecai, but of all the Jews in the Persian Empire as well.

Mordecai asks Esther to go before the king on behalf of the Jews, but anyone who goes into the inner court of the king without being called is put to death—unless the king holds out the golden scepter. It's been thirty days since the king has sent for Esther, so doing what Mordecai has asked her to do could end up getting her killed! Of course she's afraid.

There was Esther, the queen of Persia. Her every need was met, and there was nothing she desired that she couldn't have. She was safe—nothing could touch a person in such a lofty position, right? Wrong. Esther is also a Jew. The queen of Persia will be exterminated along with the rest of her people unless she does something.

"A woman is like a tea bag; you don't know her strength until she's in hot water."

NANCY REAGAN

None of us escapes it—crisis happens to all of us. As we'll see in the rest of Esther's story, the key to handling a crisis is in how we respond to it.

When Mordecai lets Esther in on Haman's evil plot, her response is basically this: "I understand this is a critical situation, Mordecai, and it's not that I don't feel your pain, but do you understand that I could be killed for doing what you ask?"

Mordecai retorts, "Wake up and smell the Persian tea, Esther. This is not just my problem or a problem for the Jewish people. This is *your* problem, too. Either way, you face death. You have no choice but to act." Then he gets her with this zinger: "And who knows but that you have come to royal position for such a time as this?" (Esther 4:14).

Aha, there's the big picture. There's the piece that had been missing. Now that Esther has that missing piece, her destiny starts to make sense. She is about to experience the very first "Esther moment."

"AHA!"…"OH NO!"

In that moment, the "aha!" is quickly followed by an "oh no!" The conversation in her head might have sounded something like this: *Aha!*

Now I see what this is all about. This position of queen isn't just so that I can sit back, eat grapes, and look pretty. God placed me here to make a difference, to play a critical role—to do something!

But right on the heels of that revelation comes this: *Oh no! Now I see how this crisis situation affects me and why God brought me to this moment. I have to use all I've learned and all I've been through to make a difference in this situation. It seems out of my control, and it demands more strength than I think I have.*

At that moment her stomach feels like it drops to the floor, and whatever blush she's wearing isn't enough to compensate for the blood that drains from her face.

The aha! brings with it the realization of a bigger picture; the oh no! puts her at a fork in the road to destiny. The question now is this: How will she respond? Daunted by the task before her, will she pull back in insecurity, only to be haunted forever by her inability to overcome her fears? Or will she trust God? Will she reach to a Source greater than herself and find the confidence of conviction needed to face what she knows she must do?

> *"I've never been one who thought the Lord should make life easy; I've just asked Him to make me strong."*
>
> EVA BOWRING

AN *E*STHER MOMENT

Nicole Johnson, Miss America 1999, had an "aha!...oh no!" type of crisis, too, and her response to that crisis, like Esther's to hers, affected not only herself, but many others as well.

When Nicole was a sophomore in college, she began feeling tired, thirsty, and hungry all the time. She figured that she was worn down because of her heavy class load. But then she also started losing weight, experiencing nausea, vomiting, blurred vision, and going to the bathroom a lot more than usual.

Her "aha!" moment came when she visited the doctor over

Thanksgiving weekend and was diagnosed with juvenile (type 1) diabetes. So that's what was causing those symptoms! But close on the heels of the "aha!" came the "oh no!" Maybe an out-of-control racist wasn't trying to exterminate her and her race, but this disease, left untreated, would kill her all the same. Her life would depend on daily insulin injections, several blood sugar checks every day, a strict diet, and mandatory daily exercise. Nicole was facing an "Esther moment." Her world had turned upside down; she was confused and depressed. How would she respond to this crisis?

Nicole's deep faith in God gave her the strength to go on. "Once I finally recovered from the initial shock of diagnosis and learned more about the disease," she says, "I adopted a can-do attitude, one that was more determined and focused than 'prediabetes.' In a very real way, the crisis of diabetes both softened my heart and toughened my resolve. It helped mold me into a person who saw a world of possibilities open up again."

By the time I met her, Nicole had participated in state preliminaries for the Miss America title a couple of times, but she had never made it all the way to the finals in Atlantic City. Others had discouraged her from participating in the pageants because of her disease and the physical toll it would take on her body, and she was about to give up on that dream. But believing that the mantle of Esther was on her, I encouraged her to try one last time. Several months later I was thrilled to watch on television as she was crowned Miss America and made that famous walk down the runway.

That title, however, was not her destiny. God positioned Nicole as Miss America 1999 to give her a platform from which to speak about an issue that affected not only her, but also thousands of others. Wearing an insulin pump all the time, Nicole spent a rigorous year traveling and educating the public about the "hidden killer" that she battles daily. She launched a diabetes awareness campaign that brought this issue to national attention, raising millions of dollars for research and improving insurance coverage for people with diabetes. One young woman's response to her crisis changed thousands of lives.

More importantly, Nicole was able to use her position to talk openly about her faith, even when she was advised not to. "I wouldn't be the person I am today had I not been diagnosed with diabetes," she says. "But I also wouldn't be the person I am today had it not been for my strong and grounded faith."

CLARITY AND CHARACTER THROUGH YOUR RESPONSE TO CRISIS

So often we think of crisis in terms of bad things happening: a failing marriage or other romantic disappointment, a life-threatening illness, the loss of a job, the death of a loved one, or some other major catastrophe. But the dictionary gives an interesting definition of *crisis*: "an unstable or crucial time or state of affairs whose outcome will make a decisive difference for better or worse." Certainly that could be said of the crisis Esther faced!

The Chinese language uses characters, or pictures, rather than words or letters to express ideas. The Chinese word for *crisis* is a combination of two characters—one meaning "danger" and the other meaning "opportunity." There definitely was danger involved in Esther's moment of crisis, but there was opportunity, too. Crisis isn't just about tragedy. Notice that part of the definition of crisis has to do with the outcome. And the outcome often depends on how we respond—the choice we make.

I have had many of the same thoughts and emotions that Esther must have had in situations where the tasks and risks seemed every bit as big to me as they probably did to her. Sometimes I made the right decision, faced my fears, stepped out in faith, and came out stronger. Other times I made the "other decision"—you know, the decision to not decide—and I chose not to choose. When we allow ourselves to be paralyzed by fear, we don't realize that the moment of crisis is also the moment of opportunity.

Oddly enough, it often takes a crisis to help us see things more clearly. A crisis has a way of eliminating unimportant or irrelevant things that clutter our lives. This is the clarity that comes from crisis. Our response to crisis also has the potential to produce or reveal faith, courage, wisdom, discernment, and humility. This is the character that comes from crisis.

As with Nicole, our response can bring clarity, strength, greater dependence on God, and even a clearer revelation of our destiny. At Esther's point of crisis, she saw clearly that there was a reason she had become queen. Once her realization that this was a moment of destiny became stronger than her hesitation—even in light of the personal sacrifice it required—her response was decisive, prayerful, and courageous.

AN *Esther* MOMENT

From the journal of a modern-day Esther:

Endure
the storm
just one more day
so you may
fully appreciate
the calm
—Lisa Dauffenbach[7]

That is the response God is looking for when we face crisis. That is the response Esther chose—she understood that it wasn't only about her. She knew that whatever happened to her, she was acting for the good of her people. "If I perish, I perish," she said bravely and put her life in God's hands.

That was also Jesus' response when He faced the most agonizing crisis in history—the cross. In the Garden of Gethsemane, He cried out, "My soul is overwhelmed with sorrow to the point of death." He fell with his face to the ground and prayed, "My Father, if it is possible, may this cup be taken from me. Yet not as I will, but as you will" (Matthew 26:38–39). Knowing that He was about to take upon Himself the sin of the world—past and future—He wrestled with God: "Isn't there any other way?" The crisis Jesus faced was about His ultimate destiny, which was to become the Savior of the world. The response He chose was to submit to the will of His Father out of love for you and me.

We have a great Savior who redeems lives in the here and now and for all eternity, but we still live in a fallen world. That's why sometimes, bad things happen. But what Satan has meant for evil, God will use for good to those who love the Lord and are called according to his purpose (Romans 8:28). The Bible certainly does not guarantee that we as Christians will escape crisis. If anything, it guarantees that we will *not* escape hard times: "In this world you will have trouble" (John 16:33). What we do have is the incredible promise that the God of the universe will be with us in our time of crisis:

> When you pass through the waters, I will be with you; and when you pass through the rivers, they will not sweep over you. When you walk through the fire, you will not be burned; the flames will not set you ablaze. For I am the LORD, your God, the Holy One of Israel, your Savior. (Isaiah 43:2–3)

Rise Up!

Yes, doo-doo happens, but with each crisis, no matter how big or small, we are faced with the choice of how we will respond. To paraphrase Shakespeare: "To act or not to act? That is the question." We can either choose to be a victim of the circumstances surrounding us and crumble, or we can rise up, face our fears head-on, and become stronger because of it. Crisis is an opportunity to respond. Our response to crisis is the key. Will you respond in hesitation and fear? Or will you respond in faith and courage *for such a time as this?*

See It, Say It, Walk It Out!

- "So do not fear, for I am with you; do not be dismayed, for I am your God. I will strengthen you and help you; I will uphold you with my righteous right hand." (Isaiah 41:10)
- "We have this treasure in jars of clay to show that this all-surpassing power is from God and not from us. We are hard pressed on every side, but not crushed; perplexed, but not in despair; persecuted, but not abandoned; struck down, but not destroyed." (2 Corinthians 4:7–9)
- "I can do everything through him who gives me strength." (Philippians 4:13)

Just Do It!

1. Think of a time when you faced a personal crisis—a fork in the road of your destiny. Looking back, you can probably see how God used that to define your character. Write down some of the things you learned about yourself through that circumstance or the ways God changed you and helped you to grow through it.

_____

_____

_____
_____
_____
_____
_____

2. Now that you have had a chance to reflect on the past, let's look to the future. Jesus says, "In the world you will have tribulation; but be of good cheer, I have overcome the world" (John 16:33, NKJV). There it is in black and white: You *will* have tribulation— but through Jesus you can overcome. Given this reality, write a "crisis statement"—three to four sentences to state how you will respond when crisis hits. Use Scripture if you'd like.

    When crisis comes, I will…

    _____
    _____
    _____
    _____
    _____
    _____
    _____

The Providential Power Source

...forsuchatimeasthis

Relief and deliverance for the Jews will arise from another place.

ESTHER 4:14

I've said before that this is a book about character. But this chapter isn't about Esther's character—it's about God's character. More specifically, it's about God's providential power. It appears here—sandwiched between the chapters on crisis and destiny—because a crisis isn't just a random happening, and without God, destiny can seem like the cruel hand of fate. God's providence holds the balance between the two.

Oddly enough, only two verses in the entire book of Esther refer to God's providence, and even those are pretty indirect. If you can believe it, of all the books in the Bible, this is the only one that never actually mentions God. Not once.

No one sees God in a burning bush or hears His voice thunder and echo, "I am God, and this is your **destiny**...**destiny**...destiny...."

No prophet announces, "God spoke to me and this is His word to you."

Monica from *Touched by an Angel* never appears with a warm, amber glow to declare, "I'm an angel and God has sent me to tell you that He loves you and has a plan for your life."

No, only two verses—Esther 4:14, 16—even hint that a sovereign hand is orchestrating all the events. Still, when you read the book of Esther, you can't help but feel that God is all over it. If you look for the clues, you begin to detect His fingerprints and notice things that He has touched. You can catch a whiff of His fragrance and know that He has been there.

LIGHTS, CAMERA...ACTION!

If you've ever taken an acting class or participated in a drama production, you've seen a director in action. He or she is the one who sets the stage, guides the action, coaches the line delivery, oversees the construction of the sets, worries about costuming, and approves lights, sound, and half a jillion other details.

The people in the audience never see the director. He never comes out for a bow at curtain call. But if they understand how drama works, they know that he's been there the entire time. They understand that he has been intimately involved in every aspect of the production, moving here, nudging there, adding his invisible signature to every part of the drama.

That's a good illustration of God's presence in the book of Esther. He's the great Director behind all the action and intrigue, the creative touch behind all the plot twists. Though He is silent, He's not unseen in the events that play out. Even in the silence, you can see His hand maneuvering events and people toward His determined outcome. He is behind the scenes, directing it all.

Sounds like something right out of a movie, doesn't it?

PICTURE THIS!

A great pageant is proclaimed throughout the land, and Esther—played by Julia Roberts with her contagious smile—is entered in the

contest. She makes it all the way to the finals at the palace and immediately finds favor with the event organizer, Hegai. Where does that
favor come from?

She is then set apart from her peers and given special treatment—
including special food and cosmetics. She leaves all her old friends
behind in what must seem like another life. But at the same time seven
choice maidens are appointed to become her new companions. Who
do you think influenced Hegai in the selection of this new circle of
friends?

After twelve months of preparation, Esther comes before the king
and receives more favor. In fact, *great* favor. Who keeps shining the
spotlight on this young starlet from such humble circumstances?

Later on, just when Haman is plotting to annihilate the Jews, who
is it that keeps the king awake half the night with insomnia? Who
keeps the king's eyes so sleepless that he asks for a history lesson to
help put him to sleep? Why does the king's reader "just happen" to turn
to those specific pages in the massive royal chronicles—pages that
remind his highness of Mordecai's unrecognized, unrewarded loyalty?
Then, in an amazing coincidence, Haman "just happens" to be walking
by when the king needs some advice on how to honor an esteemed
subject (which Haman arrogantly assumes to be himself).

Much to that proud man's humiliation, the outcome is a twist of
fate he could never have dreamed of. Remember, Haman despised
Mordecai because he wouldn't bow down to him. Can't you just see the
humiliation on Haman's face as he has to publicly honor Mordecai, a
Jew, draped in all the king's finest?

Only the Great Director could have orchestrated such delicious
irony.

Then—when it's time to get serious—Esther calls for a fast (Esther
4:16). This may be the most obvious clue pointing to God's hand in
the events in this book. As we know, Esther is a Jew. For centuries her

people had fasted and cried out for divine help in times of trouble—help from Jehovah, the God of the Jews and the God of the Bible.

Though it's never said in so many words, it's obvious that Esther, her maids, and the whole Jewish population are praying and fasting to that same God.

After a three-day fast to ask God for wisdom and favor in the battle to save His people, Esther puts on her power suit and goes for a stroll...right into the king's presence. This is an incredibly bold move because she could die for coming to the king uninvited. If the king happens to be in an irritable mood, it could easily spell the end for Esther.

But the king isn't in an irritable mood.

And it isn't the end of Esther.

He is pleased and delighted to see his young queen. He sees her in the hall, calls her in, extends his royal scepter, and she receives favor... *again.*

She breaks her fast with not one, but two big-time banquets (I've got to talk to Esther about how to break a fast) to which she invites both the king and Haman. Of course there is no way they could have refused, because it was really an invitation to a *divine* appointment. Though nobody saw Him, God was a guest at that dinner party, and He had events well in hand.

Then at the climax of the drama, Esther's words, guided by God's Spirit, bring revelation to the king. His eyes are opened, God's people are delivered once again, there's a big dramatic musical piece with full orchestra, and...(pause for effect)...fade to black. The credits begin to roll, and whose name gets top billing?

The Director.

You never saw Him or even heard His name mentioned. But who could doubt that He was there?

EVERYTHING HAPPENS FOR A REASON

This story has all the elements of a great drama: a beautiful heroine, an evil villain, conflict, crisis, climax, and conclusion. But just like a novel or a screenplay in the hands of a good writer, the end is already written (victory) and the author (God) skillfully provides the way.

Yes, crisis happens. Esther found herself in a crisis, all right. And from a human perspective, she had every reason to be afraid. But God was in control and had already provided the way out.

The word we use to describe these divinely coordinated events is *providence*. It comes from the root word to *provide,* and it means "the act of providing or preparing for future use or application; a making ready; preparation. Preparation in advance; foresight." In other words, *providence* means to provide or to make ready ahead of time, to prepare for future events.

No matter what your circumstances, God is never caught off guard. He never has to scramble around, develop contingency plans, or huddle with a crisis management team to find a solution. No. This is the God who not only knows everything, He also knows it beforehand! He has been at work preparing Esther *her entire life* for this moment. All the years of preparation—spiritual, physical, and emotional—are converging for this moment in history.

That's providence.

That's the hand of the Great Director.

This is the God to whom Esther prays and fasts. He will deliver His people—even if Esther chooses not to act with faith and courage in the face of this crisis.

AN *E*STHER MOMENT

When Psalm 33:11 speaks about "the purposes of his heart through all generations," that includes Esther's generation *and* ours. God is still at work today, writing, directing, moving behind the scenes to bring about His purpose. Let me tell you about someone you might not typically think of as a modern-day Esther. But remember that this chapter is about the character of God, and His sovereign purpose comes through loud and clear in this story. Like Esther, Jenni faced a life-and-death crisis. If she did not face her crisis, she, too, would surely die.

When Jenni was a child, her family moved around a lot, which doesn't make any child feel very secure. But on top of that general feeling of insecurity, she was sexually abused by several different men, and that stripped away any security that was left. She began to believe that there must be something wrong with her, that she was to blame, and that no one could ever love her. To numb the pain, she started using drugs and alcohol. Something inside told her that if she hurt herself, nobody else could hurt her. This warped and persistent thinking led her into an eating disorder—anorexia. She began the slow suicide of self-starvation. What she ate was the only thing in her life that she felt she could control.

But in reality, she had never been more out of control: Her body was shutting down because of the eating disorder. It left her too sick to work, so she lost the job she loved and the place where she was living. She was homeless, addicted, and losing the battle for her mind and body.

This emaciated, strung-out girl walked the streets of Sydney, Australia, knocking on the doors of rehabilitation clinics, halfway houses, and hospitals. She was turned away every time because she didn't have money or insurance. One night, near the end of her rope, Jenni lay in bed and cried out in anguish to God: "I will do whatever it takes; please just help me. I want to live!"

The very next day, some friends of hers who had read Nancy Alcorn's book *Echoes of Mercy* told her about Mercy Ministries in America. They suggested that she e-mail them to find out whether they could refer her to a Mercy home. Mind you, Mercy Ministries is not sitting around waiting for girls on the other side of the world to contact them so that they can fill up their program. There is a long waiting list, and sometimes it can take months to get in.

But God had something in mind for this young woman, and by His providence, arrangements were made for Jenni to go to America and be admitted into the "house that mercy built." To this day she doesn't know who arranged for her visa and paid for her airline ticket, but God's provision was there. Within two weeks, this hopeless, penniless, anorexic girl went from the streets of Sydney, Australia, to her new home-away-from-home in Nashville, Tennessee.

If you are a troubled young woman in crisis—unplanned pregnancy, drug or alcohol addiction, eating and emotional disorders—there is help and hope at a home called Mercy. Mercy Ministries P.O. Box 111060 Nashville, Tenn. 37222-1060 1-800-922-9131 1-615-831-6987 MercyMinistries.com

Over the next year, Jenni chose to be set apart to begin what would be a slow process of letting the walls of her heart down enough to let God's love in. It was painful to get real and honest before others, herself, and God. She had to forgive those who had hurt her and forgive herself for her own bad choices. She acknowledged that she had blamed God for the things that happened to her, but she ultimately surrendered her heart and healing into His hands. By daily transforming her mind through God's Word, she began to see herself as God does and to experience His love and acceptance.

For twelve months, Jenni uncovered the bitterness of her pain, learned to experience the sweetness of laughter again, and became the beautiful young woman she is today. (Hey, there's that twelve-month preparation time again, just like we saw in Esther's story!) Jenni has graduated from the program and is now back home, helping to open a new Mercy Ministries house in Sydney, Australia. Her favorite Scripture is 2 Corinthians 5:17: "Therefore, if anyone is in Christ, he is a new creation; the old has gone, the new has come!"

God provided a way out for Jenni, and through her response to crisis, He has revealed to her a new purpose that will change many young women's lives.

TWO VIEWS OF LIFE

God is every bit as involved in the details of *your* life as He was in the details of Esther's and Jenni's.

There was a time when I was not so keenly aware of God's providence in my life. One day seemed to just flow into the next. The activities of each day were sort of meaningless, uneventful, and, yes, even ordinary, as if life was just sort of "happening." God seemed close to me only when I drew close to Him. If something bad happened, it was "bad luck." If something good happened it was "good luck" or because *I* made it happen.

That's the way most people live their lives: totally oblivious to God's presence. To many people, God is way off in heaven somewhere and gets involved in their lives only when they cry out in desperation for His help.

Now that I am just a little bit older and wiser, I can look back and see how God has provided for and directed me at every turn, good and bad. My senses are now heightened to His guiding, and I live each day expectant of His providential hand. That makes life with Him both exciting and reassuring. Even in the ordinary times of life, God is extraordinary.

Through the eyes of faith, you can begin to see and understand that every event in your life—every meeting, every conversation, every opportunity, every setback—is part of God's loving plan for your life.

What a difference this makes! Somehow, life seems to change from black and white to Technicolor. When you find yourself in conversation with a stranger, you can pray in your heart, *Lord, why have You allowed my path to cross with this person? What would You have me learn? How can I touch this person's life for You?*

When you walk into a new class or job, you can pray, *Lord, which lives do You want me to touch for You? What truths do You have planned to teach me? How can I serve You by serving others?*

When goodness comes your way, you can thank *God* for it instead of attributing it to dumb luck or even to your own hard work. When trials come, you can ask God what He wants to show you and teach you or how He wants to glorify Himself through your responses.

What a great way to live! Instead of being aimless and arbitrary, every moment of life begins to take on purpose and meaning. You begin to sense God's hand behind even little things that touch your life…an encouraging letter from a friend, a sunset, a rainbow…or even a fender bender on a rainy day when you're late for work.☺ You no longer speak of coincidences or being lucky because you understand that the Great Director has arranged all the entrances and exits in your life.

Rise Up!

Awaken yourself to the hand of God moving in your life. He is not only in the extraordinary; He is also in the ordinary events of life. Look to the divine Director to guide your every step, word, action, and motivation as you play your part in His kingdom drama for this generation. As they say in show business, "You're on!" *for such a time as this.*

See It, Say It, Walk It Out

☼ "Many are the plans in a man's heart, but it is the LORD's purpose that prevails." (Proverbs 19:21)

☼ "I make known the end from the beginning, from ancient times, what is still to come. I say: My purpose will stand, and I will do all that I please…. What I have said, that will I bring about; what

I have planned, that will I do." (Isaiah 46:10–11)

💘 "'The decision is announced by messengers, the holy ones declare the verdict, so that the living may know that the Most High is sovereign over the kingdoms of men and gives them to anyone he wishes and sets over them the lowliest of men.'" (Daniel 4:17)

JUST DO IT!

1. 📋 Journal It:

   Ask God to reveal how He has providentially directed your life in ways you weren't even aware of. In moments of crisis, how did He "set up" your deliverance? Remember: Don't always look for a dramatic entrance; look for the subtle fingerprints of God.

   _____

   _____

   _____

   _____

   _____

   _____

   _____

   _____

2. Are you willing to be God's provision for someone else? I guarantee that God will be happy to use you in that way. He probably already is and you don't even know it. Take a few moments and ask the Lord to use you as provision in the life of someone else. Get ready though, because it will happen! ☺

chapter twelve

Destiny with a Purpose

...forsuchatimeasthis

For if you remain silent at this time, relief and deliverance for the Jews will arise from another place; but you and your father's family will perish. And who knows but that you have come to royal position for such a time as this?

ESTHER 4:14

I n Esther 4:14 we find the pivotal phrase that describes Esther's destiny: for such a time as this. Books, songs, and sermons have been written on this one phrase, inspiring individuals to ask God for insight into what He is doing through them at a particular point in time. The phrase serves as a stake driven into the timeline of history, alerting us to the destiny of the moment, a moment when events could go either way.

ESTHER'S DATE WITH DESTINY

This is the climax of Esther's story. The preparation, the process, the position, and the problem all meet at this moment. Esther is exactly the person God needs in just this place at precisely this time.

Earlier, when Mordecai sensed her hesitation, he had brought the significance of the situation to Esther's attention: "Don't you get it, Esther? This is your destiny. Perhaps you have been brought to the palace for precisely this moment."

And suddenly she gets it: There's a purpose for her being right where she is. Until now, Esther hadn't realized her part in God's eternal screenplay—that everything up to now had been preparation for her to put it all on the line at this moment. If God hadn't brought her through all He had, Esther would have been as voiceless as the masses of Jewish people scattered abroad. But now, because of His hand, she has direct access to the king. She can at least *try* to make a difference.

She must choose to rise to her destiny. This date with destiny threatens to move Esther out of her comfort zone. If she tries to help, she may have to pay the ultimate price. It's the crossroad of the "aha!"…"oh no!" moment.

Most of us are not destined to alter the course of history for an entire race. Destiny can be so difficult to understand because we tend to look for big moments—points in time where history hangs in the balance, waiting for us to act. It is much more common for a destiny to be lived out over an entire life.

LITTLE MOMENTS OF DESTINY

As a child, I watched the movie *It's a Wonderful Life* every Christmas. Year after year I would relive with George Bailey the feeling that life is passing him by—that others get to follow their dreams while he stays home, his dreams in the closet.

George dreams of building big bridges and tall buildings, but instead he is stuck working in the family business while others, including his brother, go off to make names for themselves. His brother even wins a Medal of Honor for saving many lives during World War II.

On the brink of a financial crisis that is not his fault, George concludes that his family would be better off without him—that it would be better if he'd never been born. Then an angel allows George to get a glimpse of what life would've been like without him. Because George wasn't there to save his little brother from drowning after breaking through the ice one day, his brother died as a child and wasn't able to save the lives of others during World War II. The pharmacist in the drugstore where George worked after school went to prison and afterward became a drunk because George wasn't there to stop him from making a mistake with a prescription that ultimately killed a child. His beautiful wife became an old maid because she never met George—the love of her life. The town even had a different name because George wasn't there to fight against a power hungry man.

Eventually, George understands that there's more to his life than he thought, and he begs to go home, to go back to being George Bailey.

For George, there were several crucial moments of destiny, although those events didn't seem especially noteworthy to him at the time. By getting this glimpse at what life would be like without him, George realizes that there is a purpose for his life. He comes to understand that seemingly inconsequential actions have long-term effects and are many times the evidence of a life of destiny.

George's story, of course, has a happy ending, but he doesn't know that when he decides to go back to his life. All he knows is that his life has meaning and purpose. Our ability to deal with crisis in that light can give clarity and peace—God is in control.

PREPARATION FOR DESTINY

We often think of destiny as an end, as a destination. Somehow, we have gotten the idea that we have to find that destination and that if things are going badly, we must have missed it. We do have an ultimate destiny through Christ in eternity, but personal destiny is often more than a one-time event. Many times we get confused between the preparation or the position and the destiny or the purpose.

The great thing about God being in charge of our destiny is that He can see into the future, whereas we can see things clearly only when we're looking back. God's foreknowledge means that He can see ahead and take us on the best route to where we need to go. His foreknowledge is a big part of providence: He provides before we even know what we need.

Remember the movie *Back to the Future*? Marty McFly goes back in time and ends up in high school with his parents. But his arrival in the past messes up his destiny—he lands right in the middle of the day his parents were to have met and fallen in love, and he spends the rest of the movie trying to fix it. With a lot of effort and a couple of futuristic tricks, he finally convinces his father to ask his mother to the big dance at school and to use this line: "Lorraine, you are my destiny." Of course, his poor father is so nervous that he botches it completely, telling her, "Lorraine, you are my density." But the point is this: Marty could be certain that George and Lorraine were meant to be together because he had foreknowledge.

Sometimes, a woman's destiny is simply following her natural inclinations and interests—and things just seem to fall into place. But that's rare. More often, God knows that we need a little preparation before we get to our destiny.

That's what God did when He led the Israelites out of Egypt. He could have taken them right to the Promised Land, but keep in mind that these people had been slaves for years. They knew what fear was, but sometimes the fear of the known is easier to face than the fear of the unknown. Exodus 13:17 says, "When Pharaoh let the people go, God did not lead them on the road through the Philistine country, though that was shorter. For God said, 'If they face war, they might change their minds and return to Egypt.'" So he took them the long way—which turned out to be *really* long—so that when they finally reached the Promised Land they would be good and ready to enter it.

THE PROCESS OF DESTINY

Destiny isn't an *end* as much as it is a *series of points* along a path. The points are strung together by the thread of the path. Esther's destiny was not to be queen, but what she would do through her position as queen. Personal destiny does not lie in any one position, place, or event. It's in the purpose. Position, as we talked about in chapter 8, is simply a vehicle that enables your purpose. Positions come and go. Purpose remains.

Destiny, or purpose, is what you were created for. Everything that has happened until now has been part of the process of purpose. For Esther it happened so gradually that she didn't even recognize it when it came.

Destiny is a process of choosing, narrowing, focusing. It is the act of doing, held in the tension of our decisions, and our response to crises that are the determining factors.

God used diabetes and the Miss America pageant to help Nicole Johnson along the path to her ultimate destiny. He took the sexual abuse, the drug addiction, the eating disorder, and the other losses in Jenni's life and used them for a purpose. Just like the Israelites, God took what the enemy planned to use to destroy them and turned it for good—not only for Nicole and Jenni, but for others as well. God is now using both of them in the positions He has granted them to touch the lives of other young women and to shape *their* destinies.

In my own life, God has used various circumstances—from my exhilarating experience as Miss California to our devastating financial loss—to shape my ultimate destiny. Through His favor, I'm in a position that has enabled me to write this book. As you are reading it, God might be using my words to speak to you, and you in turn might take what you've learned to touch the life of someone else. It's staggering, isn't it? God doesn't orchestrate the events of a person's life in isolation; He directs our interactions with one another so that our destinies touch the destinies of other people. Wow—what a matrix of divine purpose!

Think about the tremendous opportunity this opens for us. It's not some fatalistic concept of destiny—one in which you are waiting for a particular moment to give your life meaning—but an understanding that *today* has meaning. What you're doing right now has meaning. God is always moving us toward a specific goal: "And we know that in all things God works for the good of those who love him, who have been called according to his *purpose*. For those God foreknew he also predestined to be conformed to the likeness of his Son" (Romans 8:28–29, emphasis mine).

YOUR DATE WITH DESTINY

You can tell a lot about where you are going by looking at where you've been. God has been at work molding and shaping you throughout your life. Who you are is a direct result of where you've been. As you look at your own personal history, what events have shaped who you have become? All of those experiences have been preparation for the purpose God has for your life.

As you mentally walk through your life experiences, you will begin to see the hand of God narrowing and focusing you:

- You were born a girl, not a boy.
- God gave you certain gifts and talents.
- You were born into a specific time in history.
- All your life experiences to this point have uniquely shaped who you are.

Just as Esther was particularly equipped to have an impact on her own time and culture, so you have been prepared to affect this generation. My friend Eastman Curtis, a pastor, youth conference speaker, and author, says this about the current generation: "They don't have a rebellion problem; they have a vision problem." When God's calling, vision, and purpose are revealed, all the energy previously wasted in distractions and rebellion becomes focused and directed toward the purpose for which God created you. It's like chaos suddenly being channeled into the focus of a laser beam. Once God gets hold of you and directs that energy, look out.

This generation is rising up in radical faith, responding to the tragic school shootings in Columbine and other places with grassroots prayer movements across the country. There is strength in the faith of these young people in movements like The Call D.C., Day One, and 24/7 Prayer in Europe that hasn't been seen for decades. God is doing something special in your generation—Generation Esther. Be a part of it. Find out what God is doing in this time and where the Holy Spirit is moving, and get in line with that; your destiny will present itself.

For further self-discovery about your destiny, check out the Get into Your SHAPE study. (SHAPE: Spiritual Gifts, Heart, Ability, Personality, Experiences.) Log on to www.youthministryonline.com. Look under freebees on the sidebar for a SHAPE inventory sample. Order the complete study by going to Student Messages on top/right bar or call 949-830-4042. For the thirty-something gals secretly reading this book, go to www.pastors.com. Click on CLASS. CLASS 301 can help you narrow and focus your destiny as well. Or call 949-829-0300 to order. These are all resources from Saddleback Community Church, pastored by Rick Warren, and would make a great group study.

IN LIGHT OF THE BIG PICTURE

Jesus said that He was "about his Father's business." Even now He is seated at the right hand of the Father, ruling, reigning, managing, and expanding the kingdom of God. We're part of the family business! We should be about our Father's business, too, using the gifts and talents He has invested in us. He is a wise steward of His investments. He will not let them go to waste.

A big part of destiny is using the gifts God has given you to build up the body of Christ and impact the kingdom in ways you never imagined. There is nothing more fulfilling than knowing that you are doing what God created you for. If you are walking in that purpose, you are worshiping God.

The movie *Chariots of Fire* offers a great understanding of destiny. The main character, Eric Liddell, an Olympic runner, delivers an incredible line as he tries to describe what drives him to run. His well-intentioned sister is trying to convince him that his true destiny is to be a missionary to China—and ultimately, that is where he ends up. But Eric also knows that part of his destiny involves running, because God has so clearly gifted him. He says, "When I run, I feel God's pleasure." There is nothing more gratifying than feeling the communion of God's presence and pleasure as you use the gifts and talents He has given you to the fullest. That is destiny.

When you got to this chapter, you may have thought that you were going to learn the answer to the age-old question: "Why am I here and what am I supposed to do with my life?" Well, let me be direct. If I've learned one thing along my own path, it's this: *It's not about you.* It's about what God wants to do *through* you and *in* you. This is one of the most valuable lessons you will ever learn.

My favorite quote comes from the classic devotional *My Utmost for His Highest* by Oswald Chambers: "God is more concerned with your eternal good than your immediate gratification." God's purpose is in *who* you become, not what you become or what you do. We must evaluate everything in light of God's big picture.

I said it earlier in the chapter, but in case you missed it, I'll say it again: God's ultimate destiny for you is to conform you to the likeness of His Son (Romans 8:29). Good or bad, the things that happen to you are a part of that purpose. Your gifts, your circumstances, the lessons you learn, the lives that touch you, and the lives you touch—they are all a part of that destiny. That is why the Bible says, "We know that in *all things* God works for the good of those who love him, who have been called according to *his purpose*" (Romans 8:28, emphasis mine).

RISE UP!

In the movie *Dead Poets Society,* Robin Williams's character motivates his students with the Latin phrase carpe diem, or "seize the day." You have been called and set apart for a divine purpose, so seize the day! God is doing great things through your generation, so embrace your destiny and the destiny of Generation Esther. Who knows but that you were put in your particular circumstances with your special gifts *for such a time as this.*

SEE IT, SAY IT, WALK IT OUT

- "'For I know the plans I have for you,'" says the LORD. "'They are plans for good and not for disaster, to give you a future and a hope.'" (Jeremiah 29:11, NLT)
- "We know that in all things God works for the good of those who love him, who have been called according to his purpose. For those God foreknew he also predestined to be conformed to the likeness of his Son." (Romans 8:28–29)
- "Yet I still belong to you; you are holding my right hand. You will keep on guiding me with your counsel, leading me to a glorious destiny." (Psalm 73:23–24, NLT)

JUST DO IT!

1. Take inventory:
   Journal your answers to the following questions. Take your time, asking the Lord to reveal new things about yourself. (You may not want to try to answer them all at once.)
   - What are my strengths, my talents?
   - What makes me unique?
   - What was I good at as a child?
   - At this time in my life, what is my favorite thing to do? Second favorite?
   - If I could do one thing for the rest of my life, what would it be?
   - If I could fight one cause for the rest of my life, what would it be?
   - How have crises and God's providence shaped and directed my life?

2. Pray:
   I recently discovered an old journal of mine. More than fifteen years ago I wrote that I felt God was calling me to write and have a ministry to young women—and that is now becoming part of my realized destiny. Ask God to give you a glimpse of your destiny. Write it down and keep on writing as God brings things to mind.

   _____

   _____

   _____

   _____

   _____

   _____

Choices Matter

...forsuchatimeasthis

n each of the past three chapters we've looked at Esther 4:14, in which Mordecai presents Esther with the most frightening challenge of her life. Look again at his pointed words:

> Do not think that because you are in the king's house you alone of all the Jews will escape. For if you remain silent at this time, relief and deliverance for the Jews will arise from another place, but you and your father's family will perish. And who knows but that you have come to royal position for such a time as this? (Esther 4:13–14)

What a speech! There's the crisis, the subtle reference to God's providence, and the hint of Esther's destiny. And in the very next verse, we read how Esther responds. But what happens *between* the time Mordecai presents the dilemma and challenge and the time Esther responds? You'll notice that there isn't a Scripture reference at the beginning of this chapter. That's because what we're going to talk about in this chapter is what happens between Esther 4:13–14 and 4:15.

BETWEEN THE LINES

We know that every word, every line of Scripture is inspired by God. But the Bible is such an awesome, powerful book that sometimes you can draw inspiration from *between* the lines.

Here's what I mean.

The Bible gives us factual accounts of what certain people said or did down through the centuries. But it only rarely tells us what they were thinking, what was going on in their hearts and minds. As you put yourself in the place of those Bible characters and try to imagine what it was like to walk in their sandals, you'll begin to sense the drama that comes between the words—the choices that must be made between the dilemmas and the deeds.

That's what I mean about the drama between the verses. If we were in some sort of Bible reading program, trying to knock off our three chapters a day, we might cruise right over this passage without even thinking about it. Our eyes would jump from the dilemma in verse 14 to Esther's answer in verses 15 and 16.

We don't see or hear Esther going through the thought process, weighing the pros and cons. If Shakespeare had written the book of Esther, he might have had her deliver a lengthy soliloquy so the audience would know what was going on in her mind. Or if it were a TV movie, there might be lots of flashbacks going on as Esther realizes, *Yes! That's why all of this has happened!*

Esther was faced with the biggest decision of her young life. It was a decision that would shape her destiny...and that of her people. There had to be some soul-searching. There had to be a choice. But there's no game show music playing as the tension mounts. We don't get to hear her phone a friend, and she doesn't ask us, the audience, what she should do. We're left in limbo during this quiet moment of decision: no color, no commentary, no soundtrack, no studio audience.

How long did Esther ponder her choice? How long did she agonize? Was it minutes? hours? days? *This was a life-and-death decision.* In so many words, Cousin Mordecai had told her, "Look, sweetheart, don't think that just because you're queen bee up there in the palace you can escape this coming death sentence."

I don't know about you, but if I had been Esther in that moment, I think I might have struggled with Mordecai's words. Was there some way she could deny her heritage, live a lie, and escape the coming wrath? Couldn't things stay as they were for just a little while longer? What should she do? Should she hang on to the cushy palace life, with all the cool clothes, lavish royal perks, and sporty chariots…or sacrifice her life for her people and for the cause of justice? Everything hung on her decision. It was the million-dollar question, and Regis Philbin and the rest of the Jewish nation anxiously awaited her final answer.

Stop for a moment and think about this. This is a girl, maybe around your age, who has been brought through a bewildering series of events. Everything has been going pretty well so far, but now her cousin, who has helped to guide her through all of it, is asking something huge of her. Because she respects him and knows that he has her best interests at heart, she knows this isn't a request to be taken lightly. What would you have chosen to do?

AN *Esther* MOMENT

From the journal of a modern-day Esther:

Afraid to make a change.
  Popular opinion, persuasion,
      Walking along the middle.
  But someday you're gonna
Wake Up

The choices will be made,

not for them;

for the One who fills the void.

—Lisa Dauffenbach [8]

DECIDING AND DOING

The critical moment in anything is not the doing, but the deciding. Thinking comes before action. It's that period of limbo between the dilemma and the instant when a decision is finally made. That moment can seem like an eternity, or it can flash by in a split second. You think through the benefits, the costs, the risks, and then you must decide. You muster up the courage to choose. As much as you might like someone else to make the decision—your parents, your pastor, your friends—there are some choices only you can make. A big part of life is learning how to hear from God for yourself and make wise choices.

Why? Because choices matter.

Life hinges on choices, great and small.

The little choices you make today affect the big choices you will make in the future. Little lies lead to big lies. Petty thefts lead to stealing on a much larger scale. In the same way, small acts of self-discipline and courage that nobody ever sees may result in great feats of bravery and valor before the eyes of many. *Each and every decision affects the course of your destiny.* That's what we see in Esther: A series of choices have led her to this great, mountain-peak moment of destiny. She has chosen:

- to remain pure in body and mind;
- to discipline herself during twelve months of preparation and purification;

- to trust and submit to the leadership of her cousin, Mordecai;
- to remain teachable and open to the suggestions of Hegai, the eunuch in charge of the women;
- to take seriously the responsibility of her position as queen;
- to respond to her crisis with courage.

All of these choices have placed her in a position to achieve her destiny should she choose to walk in it. If she hadn't made all the little choices along the way, she might never have found herself in the right place at the right time to be God's woman of the hour. And Mordecai had made it clear that if she chose to give in to her fears and walk away from her destiny, God would raise up someone else and bring deliverance from another source. Whether or not we choose to answer His call, God will always accomplish His purpose.

Does that mean that we could compromise our destiny?

You bet.

God extends the offer, but the choice is ours. Choices *do* matter.

LITTLE CHOICES, LIFE CHOICES

This is a time in your life when you are making *a lot* of choices that will set your course for a lifetime.

Some choices are easy: what to eat, what to wear (okay, maybe that's not always such an easy choice). Choices based on your moral convictions and your desire to please God are more difficult to make. I'm talking about things like sexual purity, honesty in the little things, your choice of friends, honoring your parents even after you've left their home, and speaking out against injustice even when it's politically incorrect. In the very moment when Esther's destiny was revealed, she had the choice to walk in it or shrink back from it. And fear must have been a very large factor in that moment.

Have you ever found yourself dealing with that sort of fear? You might be on the very threshold of some great step toward your destiny—when Satan suddenly fills your veins with ice water. Instantly, you are terribly afraid of making a wrong choice. I can relate to this. When I was about eighteen years old, I felt completely overwhelmed with some of the life choices I was facing. I wanted so much for someone else to just make them for me. And to this day I have trouble making choices.

Don't be so worried about making right choices that you don't make any choices at all. When it comes right down to it, nobody ever runs away from a decision. The choice not to choose is still a choice. Maybe you've heard the expression "If you don't choose, life has a way of choosing for you." When you refuse to choose, you have—by default—chosen.

The simple fact is that you *will* make some poor choices along the way. Perhaps you have already. I certainly have made some bad ones and paid the price. But do you know what? Those are the lessons I tend to remember the best. If you're making no mistakes, you're not making enough choices. Just because you've muffed a decision or two doesn't mean you will miss your destiny and God's plan and purpose for your life (although it may seem like it sometimes).

Remember Peter? He made the worst decision of his life when he caved under pressure and denied His Lord—three times (Matthew 26:69–75)! What a terrible decision! He turned coward at the most crucial moment imaginable. What pain and sorrow and regret he brought upon himself! After Jesus rose from the dead, Peter had a difficult time even looking his Lord in the eye. Yet just a couple of months later, a forgiven, restored Peter—full of the Holy Spirit and power—preached boldly before a huge multitude, and thousands responded.

In time, God will work through it all—even our bad decisions—to His glory, and He will bring us back on course. It just might take longer. But God is a redeemer, and He can use those wrong choices to teach us valuable lessons that can better prepare us for His ultimate purpose and destiny in our lives. And He assures us in His Word that "in all things God works for the good of those who love him, who have been called according to his purpose" (Romans 8:28). I keep going back to this verse because it relates to so many aspects of our lives: our crises, our destinies, God's providence in our lives—and our choices.

Destiny isn't something that sneaks up on you and overtakes you. It isn't like some big wave that comes up out of the ocean and washes over you while you're building a sand castle. Any talk about fate leaves God and personal responsibility right out of the equation. In truth, destiny is a series of choices. Choices, not chance, determine destiny. Esther's choices brought her to the doorstep of her destiny, and when she needed the courage to make the biggest decision of her life, God was right there to help her.

AN *E*STHER MOMENT

Erin Buescher knows that choices matter because she made a very difficult one. This tall, exuberant modern-day Esther seemed to have everything going for her. By the time she graduated from high school, seventy colleges had recruited Erin to play basketball. She accepted a sports scholarship to a major university in California, where she became a star player on the women's basketball team. For three years in a row she not only led her university to NCAA tournament wins, but was also chosen as the Big West Conference Player of the Year. Anyone would have assumed that she was destined for a career in professional basketball.

But as Erin approached her senior year in college, she became more and more depressed. Basketball had always been her joy, but now she didn't even want to play. She knew that her destiny was more than that. While basketball was a big part of her life, it wasn't *all* of her life, and there was an empty part of her that just couldn't be filled by shooting hoops. Her mother could see that Erin wasn't happy, so she encouraged her to transfer to a smaller, Christian college—so two weeks before school started that's just what Erin did.

Some questioned the wisdom of her choice. How would she ever live out her destiny of playing professional basketball if she went off to some small school where no one would ever see her play? She'd be burying her talent! But Erin didn't see it that way. It was a difficult choice to go against the odds and against the flow, but Erin's spiritual hunger had become greater than her athletic desires. To put Erin's thoughts in Esther's terminology: *If I have to die to basketball, I am willing to die to basketball, but I have to act on my convictions and do what's right no matter what the cost.*

But God had given Erin a gift for playing basketball and, like Eric Liddell, when she used it, she felt God's pleasure. God has rewarded Erin's choice to "seek first the kingdom of God" (Matthew 6:33) by raising her to a new position of leadership. When a major talent like that shows up at a small school and that small school suddenly starts beating everyone it plays, people notice. When WNBA scouts found out why she had made this weighty decision, they respected the integrity of her choice and have kept their eye on this star player. Now the sparkle is back in Erin's crystal blue eyes, and she beams as she runs down the court, feeling God's pleasure. Something tells me she will find favor when the draft comes around.

RISE UP!

Many years before Esther made the choice that affected the destiny of her people, another Jewish leader stood before his nation and said:

> But if serving the LORD seems undesirable to you, then choose for yourselves this day whom you will serve…. But as for me and my household, we will serve the LORD. (Joshua 24:15)

The ultimate choice you can make in life is an eternal one: to receive Jesus Christ as Savior and follow Him as Lord. He will begin to speak to you through His Word and through the Holy Spirit regarding the choices you face. His Word will be a lamp to your feet and a light to your path (Psalm 119:105). This eternal choice will affect all other choices. Every choice is a piece in the puzzle of shaping your life and the woman of destiny you will become. He will give you the wisdom and boldness to make choices that produce life, not death, *for such a time as this.*

See It, Say It, Walk It Out

- ☼ "Who are those who fear the LORD? He will show them the path they should choose." (Psalm 25:12, NLT)
- ☼ "'Martha, Martha,' the Lord answered, 'you are worried and upset about many things, but only one thing is needed. Mary has chosen what is better, and it will not be taken away from her.'" (Luke 10:41–42)
- ☼ "Don't you realize that whatever you choose to obey becomes your master? You can choose sin, which leads to death, or you can choose to obey God and receive his approval." (Romans 6:16, NLT)

Just Do It!

1. 📓 Journal It:

   Have you ever had to make a difficult choice? Write about the choice and the circumstances surrounding it.

   _____

   _____

   _____

   _____

_____

_____

_____

2. I once heard someone say, "You *sometimes* learn from experience,
   but you *always* learn from reflecting on experience." Reflect on a
   choice that you made in the past that may not have been the best
   one for you. What did you learn from it?

_____

_____

_____

_____

_____

_____

_____

_____

_____

chapter fourteen

Stand in the Gap

...forsuchatimeasthis

> [Mordecai] also gave [Esther's servant] a copy of the text of the edict for [the Jews] annihilation, which had been published in Susa, to show to Esther and explain it to her, and he told him to urge her to go into the king's presence to beg for mercy and plead with him for her people.

ESTHER 4:8

E sther's biblical predecessor, Deborah the warrior, would have been proud of Esther the advocate. You may not have thought of Esther in quite this way before. Her strength may be a quiet strength, but don't let that fool you. The warrior in Esther is about to rise up.

After Mordecai's speech, Esther now realizes that this is her moment of destiny, and she chooses to take on the cause of her people. Without losing any of her grace or elegance, she becomes a bold and courageous advocate for those who cannot save themselves. She will stand in the gap, defend the defenseless, and intercede on their behalf. She will go before the highest court in the land, before her king and husband, and fight for the cause of justice regardless of the cost.

Wow! Esther not only has character; she's got guts. It's almost a David-and-Goliath picture. Here's sweet little Esther standing up to Haman, the Jew hater, and taking a stand against religious and racial prejudice.

153

An Advocate at Any Age

How many times have you seen someone mistreated, teased, or laughed at just because he or she is different? Injustice of any kind requires an advocate. Whether it's racism, religious discrimination, or just plain meanness, God is looking for those who will stand in the gap.

I remember my very first Esther moment. It might not seem like much now, but I still recall it vividly. I was in elementary school. There was a boy in my class who was a little different—odd, actually. He was a very bright boy, but he just didn't fit in. Because of his aloof and sometimes antagonistic behavior, the other kids often made fun of him and teased him. I'm ashamed to say that I joined in. But at seven years old, this was going to be one of my first tests of character.

Bobby played alone at recess and sat alone at lunch, and no one wanted to sit by him in class. The other kids were afraid of him, and I was, too. He lived about a block from my house, so we walked the same street to and from school. He always walked alone on the other side of the street.

One day on the playground I noticed him playing by himself in the dirt. Strangely, my heart was filled with compassion as I watched him. Remember the "aha!"…"oh no!" of an Esther moment? Well, here it was: "Aha!" For the first time I saw him as a misunderstood, awkward, lonely boy; for the first time I felt the pain he must have felt when the other kids teased him; for the first time I felt the injustice. Something was telling me to go over and play with him. "Oh no!" I couldn't do that. I would most certainly face rejection from the other kids, and then I'd be playing alone and getting teased. Fear and courage played tug-of-war inside of me. Besides that, I was a girl. Everybody knows that girls don't have to be nice to boys. They have cooties, right? So why me?

I realize now that even at that young age, a battle between the flesh and the spirit was raging. Why couldn't I just *feel* compassionate without having to actually *be* compassionate? The pit in my stomach answered that question. I knew what I had to do, but could I do it? I was sure that all eyes were on me. Though apprehensive, I worked up the courage to walk over to him and say hi. As I walked, I wondered what I would do if he acted strange or didn't receive my gesture of friendship. Then I'd be doubly rejected. Too late. I was committed and had to take that chance. This wasn't about me or him anymore; it was about something bigger. It was about character, compassion, and doing the right thing.

I knelt down beside him and began to draw in the dirt with a stick. He looked up at me a little perplexed. I smiled at him and said, "Hi." He smiled back. We didn't say much, just played there in the dirt together till the bell rang. A bond of acceptance had been forged. After that, I tried to reach out and be nice to him when others weren't. Yes, I took some teasing from the other kids, but I knew I had done the right thing.

SOME THINGS NEVER CHANGE

As King Solomon said, "There is nothing new under the sun." Just like the kids in my school, Haman wouldn't tolerate anyone who was different, and many people today won't either.

Haman's hatred for the Jews had been passed down for generations. He was a descendant of Agog, king of the Amalekites, who had a history of ethnic cleansing of Israelites but had been defeated by King Saul (1 Samuel 15). Haman's ancestors hated the Jews, and so did he. The Jews were different, and Haman convinced the king that they shouldn't be tolerated. Listen to Haman as he makes his argument before the king: "They're different; we should not tolerate them" (see Esther 3:8).

Haven't you heard those same words spoken in our culture today? Despite a lot of talk about "tolerance," there's very little tolerance of Christians. We think differently. We live differently. But perhaps worst of all, we try to have an influence and an impact on those around us. So people say, "They're different. We should not tolerate them."

Working for *The 700 Club* keeps me very informed on current cultural issues and how they affect us as Christians. I'm sorry to report that we are living in a culture that is increasingly intolerant of Christians, our values, and our right to express our faith. Every day I hear stories about people who are being denied their rights, arrested, fired, physically assaulted, and even killed for simply bowing their heads, carrying a Bible, speaking the name of Jesus Christ, or boldly stating while staring down the barrel of a gun, "Yes, I believe." The battle is very real, and it's being fought all around us—in schools, in the workplace, in the privacy of our homes, even in the halls of our nation's capitol.

Haman wasn't content to hate the Jews on his own—no, he wanted to have his bigotry officially sanctioned, so he got the king to pass a law against them. Clever, huh? And that's just what's happening today, right here in our country. It's not enough for people to not tolerate Christians—they're taking them to court and trying to use the law to make the intolerance official.

A misunderstanding or distortion of "separation of church and state" has led to an all-out war to prevent any acknowledgment of God in the public forum. Did you know that those words aren't even in the Constitution? High-ranking officials and lawyers have used that phrase in the context of the First Amendment, but it simply isn't there.

Here's what the First Amendment says:

Congress shall make no law respecting an establishment of religion, or prohibiting the free exercise thereof; or abridging the freedom of speech, or of the press; or the right of the people peaceably to assemble, and to petition the Government for a redress of grievances.

Do you see anything there that would make it illegal or unconstitutional for a high school student to lead her school in prayer at the beginning of a football game? I don't. And neither did Marian Ward, but her intention to do just that got her into a lot of hot water with her school district.

AN *Esther* MOMENT

A legal case had been brewing in Marian's community for some time, and a circuit court judge had ruled that prayer at graduation and athletic events was a legal offense. Guidelines were established for such events that put religious speech in the same category as cursing, calling it offensive language.

Despite the ruling, the student body at Marian's high school had taken a vote in the spring before her senior year to decide whether *they* wanted an inspirational pregame message given by a student, and, if so, who that student would be. An overwhelming majority voted yes— they wanted an inspirational message. Marian was chosen as the alternate to deliver it.

However, when school started again in the fall, rumors were flying around that there might be problems if they actually allowed the message they had voted for. The girl who had been chosen to give it became fearful of the controversy and asked Marian to step in for her.

Sure enough, Marian was called in to the principal's office, where the principal and school superintendent made her aware of the guidelines: There was to be NO prayer, NO blessing, NO invocation, and NO reference to a deity. Um…where's the inspiration, exactly, in a speech without those things? They wanted to see a copy of what she was going to say to make sure that no laws would be broken.

Two days before the first game, Marian was approached by three of her teachers. One of them was a Christian, and she told Marian not to pray. "Don't rock the boat," she said. For Marian, who respected her teachers (this Christian teacher in particular), this situation was pretty confusing. Should she listen to what the teachers were saying? Or should she follow her own convictions, which had been shaped, in part, by what these teachers had taught her?

The day before the game the principal spoke with Marian again. This time he told her that it was her decision whether or not to show him a copy of her speech, which was a good thing, since Marian hadn't yet decided what she was going to say. However, he also warned her that it was his responsibility to enforce the rules and that there would be penalties if she disobeyed.

Be informed about your free speech and religious rights. Log on to www.aclj.org or www.saferschools.org. Knowledge is power.

Marian went about the rest of her day amid whispers and rumors about what might happen to her if she prayed: detention, suspension, not being allowed to graduate, prison. It all began to feel very real and very scary. This was definitely an Esther moment.

By this time, Marian, with the blessing of her parents, had retained an attorney who specialized in constitutional law. He advised them to file a restraining order so that Marian couldn't be arrested while they were waiting for a judge's ruling. Just hours before the game and the much-anticipated speech, this judge ruled that she had a right to free speech and that the school could not punish her. Marian was flooded with relief; she wanted to do what was right, but she didn't want to openly disobey the law.

That night, in front of a packed stadium, Marian stood at the microphone and began her speech:

Since a very good judge who was using a lot of wisdom ruled this afternoon that I have freedom of speech tonight, I am going to take it…. *Dear Lord, thank You for this evening. Thank You for all the prayers that were lifted up this week for me. I pray that You will bless each and every person here tonight—especially those involved in the game—that they will demonstrate good sportsmanship, Lord, and that we will have safety with all involved…. Bless this evening, and be with each and every one of us as we go home to our respective places tonight. In Jesus' name I pray, amen.*

The crowd erupted in applause at the simple prayer of a very courageous girl. Marian, like Esther, had stood in the gap. Marian had stood against those who want Christians to be silent. And she continued to pray before games throughout that season. The school has since banned all student-led speeches before games, but it's not over. Now in college, Marian continues to fight this legal battle for free speech and freedom of religion.

Marian Ward attributes her success in and preparation for her Esther moment to the time she set apart to attend a program held each summer in Washington, D.C.:

Leadership Training Institute of America

P.O. Box 2935

Fayetteville, AR 72702

www.uark.edu

Director, Pat Briney

lti@usa.com

501-443-0510

A VERY REAL BATTLE

Are we to passively stand by and do nothing as religious persecution and intolerance press in on us? Are we to stand by and let the Hamans of this world succeed in their injustice and hatred? Esther didn't. Marian Ward didn't.

Persecution in this country is real, but it pales in comparison to the suffering of those who belong to Jesus in other parts of the world. Make no mistake: This is a battle, and persecution against Christians is very real. Some are tortured to convert to Islam. Many more have their arms or legs cut off. Men, women, and children are forcibly circumcised without any medication, and many are gunned down or burned to death. Unless we stand in the gap, it will only get worse. We must take up the cause of our brothers and sisters in Christ.

To find out more about the persecuted church around the world, go to the Web site of Voice of the Martyrs at www.perse-cution.com. Also, to read some incredible stories of men, women, and children standing up for their faith, check out Jesus Freaks by Voice of the Martyrs and DC Talk.

There is no more powerful weapon in a battle than prayer. Appealing to the highest court—the court of heaven and the King of kings—through intercessory prayer is where the battle is won. We merely walk it out here on earth. I believe that this is part of Esther's purpose in prayer and fasting. "For our struggle is not against flesh and blood, but… against the spiritual forces of evil in the heavenly realms" (Ephesians 6:12). Esther had battled in the heavens before she ever went before her king, and we can, too. As it says in Hebrews 10:39: "But we are not of those who shrink back and are destroyed, but of those who believe and are saved." Don't shrink back. Stand in the gap through prayer. Be an advocate in intercession and action.

RISE UP!

Esther seized the moment—the Esther moment—and took action regardless of the consequences. Will you be an advocate against injustice and persecution? Jesus is your advocate. He goes before the Father and pleads your case, exonerating you of sin and opening the door of reconciliation between you and the Father. Can you do any less? Do you have the courage to be an advocate against injustice of all kinds, in action and in prayer, to intercede and stand in the gap *for such a time as this?*

SEE IT, SAY IT, WALK IT OUT

- "Remember those earlier days after you had received the light, when you stood your ground in a great contest in the face of suffering…. So do not throw away your confidence; it will be richly rewarded. You need to persevere so that when you have done the will of God, you will receive what he has promised." (Hebrews 10:32, 35–36)

- "If the world hates you, keep in mind that it hated me first. If you belonged to the world, it would love you as its own. As it is, you do not belong to the world, but I have chosen you out of the world. That is why the world hates you." (John 15:18–19)

- "Blessed are you when men hate you, when they exclude you and insult you and reject your name as evil, because of the Son of Man. Rejoice in that day and leap for joy, because great is your reward in heaven. For that is how their fathers treated the prophets." (Luke 6:22–23)

- "But rejoice that you participate in the sufferings of Christ, so that you may be overjoyed when his glory is revealed. If you are insulted because of the name of Christ, you are blessed, for the Spirit of glory and of God rests on you. If you suffer, it should not be as a murderer or thief or any other kind of criminal, or even as a meddler. However, if you suffer as a Christian, do not be ashamed, but praise God that you bear that name." (1 Peter 4:13–16)

JUST DO IT!

1. Journal It:

   Describe an injustice you have witnessed or experienced yourself. Was it religious or racial prejudice/discrimination? Was it mean-spirited teasing that alienated someone because he or she was different? How did that situation make you feel? What do you think Jesus would have done? What did you do?

   _____

   _____

   _____

   _____

   _____

   _____

   _____

   _____

   _____

   _____

Fasting and Prayer

...forsuchatimeasthis

Then Esther sent this reply to Mordecai:
"Go and gather together all the Jews of Susa and fast for me.
Do not eat or drink for three days, night or day.
My maids and I will do the same."

ESTHER 4:15–17, NLT

At this point, Esther's destiny has been revealed, and she realizes that sitting quietly and hoping that the crisis will pass is not an option. She's ready to stand in the gap on behalf of the Jews, but she knows that she can't do it in her own power. So she calls on her people and her handmaidens to fast and pray.

Esther sends out a 911 emergency appeal to all the Jews. In effect it says, "Pray as you've never prayed before! Cancel all your appointments, and don't do *anything* for the next three days—and that includes eating and drinking—but fall on your faces before God! I'm going to be doing the same thing here in the palace with my handmaidens. Everything is at stake!"

Don't eat or drink for three days? Is she crazy? There was a time in my life when the first thing I would have done in a crisis was run to the nearest Dunkin' Donuts to gorge on some comfort food. And if I had

had access to the food in Esther's royal pantry, I could have done some serious compulsive eating damage! But not Esther.

WHY DID ESTHER FAST?

Being a good Jewish girl, Esther knew the history of her people. From the time she learned her Aleph-Beth-Gimels, she would have been able to recite how the God of Israel had unleashed His mighty power and delivered His people when they fasted and cried out to Him.

Until that moment, Esther had been relying on Mordecai's guidance, but now the baton of spiritual authority had passed to her. In those moments between crisis and choosing, she had become a leader. Knowing what a dangerous situation she and her people faced, Esther fasted and prayed for:

- wisdom and direction on how to proceed;
- protection and deliverance from the enemy;
- evil, hidden motives to be exposed;
- freedom and justice for all the Jews in the empire;
- boldness to approach the king;
- favor in the king's sight so that he would invite her in and hear her requests.

Despite her favor and position, Esther knew that, like so many that had gone before her, she needed the help and wisdom that comes only through prayer and fasting. Eating herself into oblivion wasn't going to help, and she knew it. This was no time to be distracted by dipping into the cookie jar or rummaging through the fridge for munchies. She fasted because she needed to set everything else aside and cry out to God for power in her moment of crisis.

No doubt in your walk through life, you'll experience times when you need that power, too. Do you need guidance and direction as you make life decisions? Do you feel a need to be more sensitive to God's plan for your life? Saving an entire race of people may not be your destiny, but your purpose in the kingdom is no less important in God's eternal plan. He may call you to a time of fasting during those crucial destiny-shaping moments on your journey.

FASTING LINKED TO PRAYER

Fasting has nothing to do with the self-serving motives of dieting. When we fast, we are inviting God's supernatural presence into our crisis. In *You Are Not What You Weigh*, Lisa Bevere notes: "The world has perverted and reduced the fast, diminishing it to a diet. A diet may change the way you look, but a fast will change the way you live. A diet may change your appearance, but a fast will change the way you see." Fasting that gets the Lord's attention must be linked with prayer that comes right from the heart. Fasting without prayer is at best going through religious motions. At worst, it's an eating disorder.

There are several biblical purposes for fasting, and one of the most common is the one we find in the book of Esther: presenting a deeply felt request before God in a time of crisis—a prayer of petition. When you're facing a for-such-a-time-as-this moment in your life and you don't know what to do, you realize that you need divine intervention. You need God to step into your life and make a difference.

That's what fasting does. It helps us tune out distractions and lock our attention on heaven. The focus of a fast is to set aside our own will and appetites in order to hear from God and invite Him to supernaturally intervene in our situation. Esther understood the importance of shutting out absolutely everything except her pleas to God for help and guidance. Have you ever said or heard someone else say, "I can't even think about eating right now with this problem on my mind"? In such times, forget about eating—focus on getting help from the only source with the power to save.

A HUMBLE BEGINNING

Nothing is more humbling than being in a situation you can't control and knowing that you can't do anything about it by yourself. When Esther heard about the empire-wide decree against her people, she didn't act like everything was cool and she'd be "just fine." She understood immediately that the only thing to do was to humble herself before God and fast in order to seek His guidance. Her humility led her straight to God.

I don't know about you, but many times when I'm faced with a difficult situation, I'm tempted to try out a couple of things on my own before I turn to God. And when I do look to God for help, it's often to ask Him to help me carry out a solution I've come up with myself.

But Esther didn't do that. She didn't formulate a plan and then pray and fast to get God's blessing on it. She didn't say, "Listen, here's my plan. I'll throw a couple of banquets for the king and Haman to soften them up. Then I'll surprise them by telling them that with this law they've passed, they're going to kill me. Pray that this will work."

Even armed with the knowledge that God was on her side and the confidence that He would help her, Esther didn't barge into the king's presence with a list of demands. No, she came humbly, honoring his position of authority (Esther 5:1–3).

Again, Esther sets the example. That's exactly how we should come before God with our requests: in humility, honoring His position of power and authority. A godly fast with pure motives is an act of *humility* on our part, demonstrating that we understand our great need of help from heaven.

HOW TO FAST

Maybe you've thought about fasting to get clarity about God's will. But what do you do and how do you do it? The Bible is clear about what we should do—and what we shouldn't do—when we fast. The first thing you need to know is how *not* to fast.

> "When you fast," Jesus said, "don't make it obvious, as the hypocrites do, who try to look pale and disheveled so people will admire them for their fasting. I assure you, that is the only reward they will ever get. But when you fast, comb your hair and wash your face. Then no one will suspect you are fasting, except your Father, who knows what you do in secret. And your Father, who knows all secrets, will reward you." (Matthew 6:16–18, NLT)

In other words, if you decide to go on a food fast for a while, take a shower, fix your hair, put on a little makeup, and wear your favorite shirt. Just be normal! If your girlfriends are going out to lunch, it might be better to gracefully bow out than to explain why you're not eating.

Isaiah really cuts to the chase when He speaks of those who want to look spiritual but have the wrong motives. "They act so pious!… They love to make a show of coming to me and asking me to take action on their behalf. 'We have fasted before you!' they say. 'Why aren't you impressed? We have done much penance, and you don't even notice it!'" (Isaiah 58:2–3, NLT). God is never impressed when someone goes through the religious motions when she doesn't have a heart to match. He isn't just looking for an act of obedience; He's looking for a genuine heart.

Once your heart is prepared, you can decide from what to fast. Esther's fast was a full three-day fast. No food. No water. That sounds pretty extreme, but there have been even more drastic fasts than that. After Jesus was baptized, He fasted from all food for *forty days* in the wilderness before Satan tempted Him (Matthew 4). Moses and Elijah each fasted forty days before they experienced the awesome and immediate presence of God (Exodus 24:18; 34:28; 1 Kings 19:8).

While these are incredible examples of sacrifice (with equally incredibly results), I don't recommend a full fast for young women (see sidebar). Instead, let me ask you this: *What do you crave?*

Going without food altogether can too easily throw off your brain chemistry and lead to an eating disorder. Julia Ross, a clinical psychologist and the executive director of Recovery Systems (a California clinic that treats eating and weight disorders) points out in <u>The Diet Cure</u> *that changes in brain chemistry begin to occur within seven hours of an extreme low calorie intake. This change in brain chemistry affects serotonin levels and can lead to depression and possibly even initiate an eating disorder. I have personally dealt with the pain and obsession of anorexia and bulimia and don't want to send anyone else down that road.*

Do you crave desserts or chocolates? How about salty, starchy foods like chips, fries, or pizza? Or are there times when you'd like nothing better than a Big Mac and supersized fries? What about carbonated or diet drinks, coffee or tea? Some of us can't begin our day without that triple vanilla cream espresso or latte. All of us can identify with such cravings, can't we? We consume these things by habit—sometimes because we're hooked.

You may have tamed your tummy but have some other vices that are hard to walk away from. Maybe its soap operas, fashion magazines, Internet chat rooms, music, or talking on the phone with friends. What about your boyfriend? Could you both go three days or even a week without seeing or talking to each other to show God that *He* is your priority and to seek *His* presence?

What would be a real sacrifice for you to give up for a few days, a week, or even a month? If you're human, chances are that something has leaped into your mind already. If not, then pray about it, and God will reveal it to you. Trust me: He really will.

Daniel did a partial, or modified, fast. We're told that he "had been in mourning for three weeks. All that time I had eaten no rich food or meat, [and] had drunk no wine" (Daniel 10:2–3, NLT). That would mean eating mostly vegetables, whole grains, maybe some fruit, and lots of pure water to drink. And what happened to Daniel during his fast? He was given great visions from the Lord, was visited by angels, and enjoyed "great favor" with God just as Esther did.

Daniel's fast is certainly an acceptable alternative. What would it mean in today's terms? It might look something like this: no meat, no processed foods, no dairy, no Coke, nothing "white"—like sugar, salt, or white flour. Try Daniel's fast for a day or two. Yes, you may find yourself hungry for the things you're missing. But think about the incredible increase in appetite for spiritual things you'll have. When you get hungry, feed on the Word. Hunger after God and let Him satisfy you. As Jesus told His disciples: "You're blessed when you've worked up a good appetite for God. He's food and drink in the best meal you'll ever eat" (Matthew 5:6, *The Message*).

AN *E*STHER MOMENT

Heroes of the Bible aren't the only ones who have fasted and seen results from it. One young Asian-American modern-day Esther tells her story:

I grew up in a family where emotions were never expressed, as is common in the Asian culture. But even worse, women had no value in our culture. I grew up being constantly compared to my older brother, especially by my father. From elementary school until high school, negative feelings and emotional turmoil defined my relationship with my father.

Then, during my sophomore year of high school, my father went on a business trip that continues to this day.

Though his absence at first put a financial strain on us, it also brought relief. I didn't have to fear coming home from school; I didn't have to worry about my father's unpredictable moods.

Slowly, his absence created in me a sense of fatherlessness. I cried countless nights because although I knew I had a father, I felt orphaned. Then just when this feeling of fatherlessness was at its peak, God divinely orchestrated an incident that changed my view of who I was to my ultimate Father.

When I was a senior in high school, I was nominated to the homecoming court. For most girls this was an exciting thing, but I was sad because the other girls would be escorted by their fathers. As they crowned the queen and I was crowned a princess the night of the big game, God spoke to me.

He said, *What am I to you?*

In my mind, I answered him: *You're my King.*

Then I heard Him say, *And what are you?*

I responded, *I'm your daughter.*

And then, as I stood there with that crown on my head, He said to me, *Doesn't that make you a princess?*

Recently I was on *The Turning Tour* in America that promoted God's desire to reconcile fathers and children. As we were traveling, I shared my homecoming princess story around the nation. I was sure of who I was in the Lord, but every time I told the testimony, my heart ached for my earthly father. Then the Lord put it on my heart to fast for forty days.

I wanted to see my family restored. I wanted my fatherless father to know the truth of who he was in the heavenly Father's eyes. I wanted to rebuild our family by throwing away old hurts and feelings of abandonment.

I had fasted on my own before, but this time it was important that the entire family do it together. My mom decided to fast from lunch. My brother decided to fast from an Internet game that he was hooked on. And I, being the meat lover that I am, decided to fast from meat. Though the offerings seemed small, we knew that God was delighted and was going to honor our prayers.

As we continued on the tour, there were times when I was tired and hungry for some "real" food. Seeing this, Jesse, a friend of mine, would say, "Wow, isn't it worth it! Just imagine seeing your family restored!" And it *was* worth it.

Then one morning I woke up to the phone ringing. It was my dad! I had not heard from him in a year. The entire family took turns that morning talking to him and filling him in on our lives. We had just passed the halfway point of our forty-day fast.

We continued the fast with much encouragement. After we were done, we knew we had taken a step toward what God was intending for our lives…. It's a process, and we're still going to fast and pray for God's awesome plan for our family.

RISE UP!

God is still looking for young Esthers who are willing to set everything aside to seek His face and pray for His divine intervention. Do you need God's wisdom, guidance, direction, protection, favor, or deliverance in your life? And what would happen if an entire generation of Esthers came together collectively to fast and pray for this nation and for the spiritual awakening of their peers? Might we see a move of God that would rock the world? Nothing is impossible with God! Fast and pray *for such a time as this.*

See It, Say It, Walk It Out

🔆 "I proclaimed a fast, so that we might humble ourselves before our God and ask him for a safe journey…. So we *fasted* and petitioned our God about this, and he answered our prayer." (Ezra 8:21, 23, emphasis mine)

🔆 "Then I set my face toward the Lord God to make request by prayer and supplications, with *fasting*…." (Daniel 9:3, NKJV, emphasis mine)

🔆 "So He said to them, 'This kind [of stronghold] can come out by nothing but prayer and *fasting*." (Mark 9:29, NKJV, emphasis mine)

Just Do It!

1. Fast for three days regarding a personal situation: the salvation of a family member or friend, some struggle that you or a friend are going through, a decision you are facing, reconciliation of a relationship, deliverance, favor, or protection.

2. Pray:
   Lord, this week I'm going to fast from _____ *for three days. In place of that I'm going to pray for* _____ _____, *and I anticipate Your answer.* Expect it!

3. 📓 Journal It:
   What did God do or show you about this situation during your fast? How did He speak to you?

   _____

   _____

   _____

   _____

_____
_____
_____
_____
_____
_____
_____
_____
_____
_____
_____

Now Serving: Hospitality and Other Side Dishes

...forsuchatimeasthis

Esther answered, "If it pleases the king, let the king and Haman come today to the banquet that I have prepared for him."

ESTHER 5:4, NKJV

Three days have passed, and Esther, her handmaids, and the entire surrounding Jewish population haven't had anything to eat or drink. Esther has been seeking an answer to the crisis her people are facing, and an idea comes to her. Mind you, it's not an idea she came up with herself. It's the answer to all the prayers that have been going up for three days.

"Esther, give a banquet for the king."

A banquet, huh? Sounds like a great idea, Esther thinks. *I'm starving! Uh, but how…?*

"Esther, give a banquet for the king. And invite Haman."

Haman? Isn't that the guy who wants to kill me? Hmm…maybe the hunger is making me delirious.

This idea must have seemed about as crazy as telling the Israelites that they would conquer Jericho by marching around the walls of the city seven times. How on earth is a dinner party going to save the Jews from being killed? Esther doesn't know, but she has committed herself into God's hands, and she starts planning the menu.

But Esther's banquet preparation is about more than just a great dinner party....

HERE'S AN ENTERTAINING THOUGHT

Esther isn't just entertaining. Hospitality is about more than being the next Martha Stewart—cooking gourmet meals, setting a fabulous table, coordinating the flowers, and being the perfect hostess. If that's what we think it's about, we've missed the point.

> *"Hospitality is so much more than entertaining. To me, it means organizing my life in such a way that there's always room for one more, always an extra place at the table or an extra pillow and blanket, always a welcome for those who need a listening ear. It means setting aside time for planned fellowship and setting aside lesser priorities for impromptu teas and gatherings."*
>
> EMILY BARNES

If you look up the word *hospitality* in a dictionary, you'll find references to being warm, kind, generous, and receptive to guests and strangers. But you won't find any mention of food. (Go ahead, look it up. I'll be waiting here when you get back.) ☺

Can it be that hospitality isn't about the food? Perhaps sharing a meal or a batch of cookies is simply a means to opening the door for relationship. Hospitality is disarming because it means you have to reach out to another person, and when your arms are open, you're vulnerable.

Why did Esther draw the king out of his realm, the throne room, and into hers, the dining room? Was she trying to manipulate his emotions with a meal—as in "the way to a man's heart is through his stomach"? No, that kind of ulterior motive wouldn't be in keeping with the woman of character and virtue we've come to know.

Through an act of hospitality, Esther welcomes him into her personal domain, making herself vulnerable not only to her king, but also to her husband. The issue Esther has to bring before the king is a heart matter, not just a head matter. And to get to his heart, she has to open hers.

TRUE HOSPITALITY

I have seen this same gift of hospitality at work in the lives of three of my best friends. Maria can whip up a gourmet dinner out of an empty pantry on a moment's notice and get her spontaneously invited guests working and laughing together in the process. Karen can throw a party like nobody's business, drawing strangers together into some crazy game that breaks the ice and forges new friendships. And no matter when you stop by Kim's house, it always seems like she was *expecting* you as she pours the tea that was whistling in the kettle as you rang the doorbell. At least that's the way it seems to me.

To find out more about what it means to practice hospitality, check out We Didn't Know They Were Angels: Discovering the Gift of Christian Hospitality *by Doris Grieg.*

Hospitality is not a frivolous waste of time and energy, and it's not just about baking cookies. Hospitality is the loving, creative, sacrificial expression of a Christlike attitude, and it's the way the Lord uses these friends of mine to touch the hearts and lives of their family, friends, and community. Hospitality puts others before itself. Hospitality chooses to give rather than receive. Hospitality invests in relationships. Whether it's a note of encouragement, a thoughtful deed, or a smile, the power of hospitality is in serving others.

Your home doesn't have to be decorated like a magazine cover, and you don't have to own a full set of china before you can extend hospitality. It is only by giving of yourself—your *real* self—that you can get real with others. And it makes others want to get real with you.

Christian hospitality is so vital to our lives that Jesus Himself gave a powerful example at the Last Supper. With kindness, humility, and meekness, He served the disciples by washing their feet and ensuring that all the preparations were made for celebration of the Passover meal. This was the eve of His own personal crisis, yet He chose to invest His time in a meal—a celebration—as a way to remind His disciples that they had to be both servants and hosts to those who desire to enter the kingdom of God:

> *"The spirit of hospitality, you see, can thrive in the humblest circumstances. It's a matter of opening our lives to others...giving them the best we have to offer, but never allowing elaborate preparations to substitute for the sharing of the spirit of true hospitality."*
>
> EMILY BARNES

"In this world the kings and great men order their people around, and yet they are called 'friends of the people.' But among you, those who are the greatest should take the lowest rank, and the leader should be like a servant. Normally the master sits at the table and is served by his servants. But not here! For I am your servant. You have remained true to me in my time of trial. And just as my Father has granted me a Kingdom, I now grant you the right to eat and drink at my table in that Kingdom. (Luke 22:25–30, NLT)

SPIRITUAL FOOD FIGHT

I have often wondered why God would have Esther throw a dinner party at this critical point in the story. When the going gets tough, the tough start cooking—is that it? I don't think so.

Esther's hospitable disposition was as much a part of who she was as the other character traits we've seen in her: purity, inner beauty, obedience, responsibility, self-discipline, self-sacrifice, faith, and courage. What she's really serving up is a feast of the fruit of the Spirit—a regular buffet of character. The main course is hospitality, the side dishes are gentleness, humility, graciousness, and kindness, and all are seasoned with patience, wisdom, temperance, and self-control. The characteristics of virtue and the fruit of the Spirit are all part of the expression of hospitality.

> Therefore, as God's chosen people, holy and dearly loved, clothe yourselves with *compassion, kindness, humility, gentleness and patience*. Bear with each other and forgive whatever grievances you may have against one another. Forgive as the Lord forgave you. And over all these virtues put on *love*, which binds them all together in perfect unity. (Colossians 3:12–14, emphasis mine)

> The *fruit of the Spirit* is love, joy, peace, patience, kindness, goodness, faithfulness, gentleness and self-control. (Galatians 5:22, emphasis mine)

That sounds like Esther.

Time and time again Esther says, "If it please the king." She never presumes and always defers, expressing respect through kindness, humility, graciousness, gentleness, patience, temperance, self-control. This is the woman who first touched the king's heart, and now she will touch his heart once again.

Haman, however, is the opposite of Esther. Do you know what comes right before those wonderful passages about the fruit of the Spirit and virtue? In both cases, there is a list of traits that belong to a sinful nature—and they all sound a lot like our villain, Haman.

> Put to death, therefore, whatever belongs to your earthly

nature: sexual immorality, impurity, *lust, evil desires and greed, which is idolatry. Because of these, the wrath of God is coming.* You used to walk in these ways, in the life you once lived. But now you must rid yourselves of all such things as these: *anger, rage, malice, slander,* and filthy language from your lips. (Colossians 3:5–8, emphasis mine)

The acts of the sinful nature are obvious: sexual immorality, impurity and debauchery; *idolatry* and witchcraft; *hatred, discord, jealousy, fits of rage, selfish ambition, dissensions, factions and envy;* drunkenness, orgies, and the like. I warn you, as I did before, that those who live like this will not inherit the kingdom of God. (Galatians 5:19–21, emphasis mine)

Haman is evil, but God never fights evil with evil. In fact, the book of Esther gives an incredible example of how God overcomes evil with good.

WHAT A DIFFERENCE A DAY MAKES

When the king offered to give Esther the desire of her heart, why didn't she just present her case and plead for his mercy? What made her hesitate? Another banquet seems a bit over the top, don't you think? She'll have to go to all that trouble again tomorrow—a new menu (you can't serve leftovers), new flowers, a whole new theme and color scheme.

What was the point? I would have said, "Go for it now, Esther. Don't wait. You may not get this chance again." But in a flash of discernment, Esther bit her tongue and exercised two more virtues: patience and self-control. Something about the situation wasn't quite right, so Esther was willing to wait.

Self-control—now *that* can be a hard one for us girls. I'm still learning that virtue myself. Remember what we learned about feminine brainpower? Females often have a need to talk. But sometimes, in our need to communicate, we talk too much or at the wrong time. At times we speak when we should remain silent. Have you ever run off at the mouth about something, only to regret that you didn't have more self-discipline over your mouth? There is a "time to be silent and a time to speak" (Ecclesiastes 3:7), and it takes a lot of wisdom to know the difference!

How did Esther have the discernment to know that the timing wasn't right? Discernment is a reflection of wisdom and a sensitive spirit. Esther was probably still observing the fast she had called to ask for wisdom, discernment, God's favor, and victory in the battle. The Bible says that if we ask for wisdom, God will give it to us (James 1:5).

The king must have been perplexed when she said, "I've invited you all here to invite you all here again tomorrow. Same time, same place." Esther had no way of knowing, but in just twenty-four hours, nothing would be the same.

Haman leaves the first banquet feeling pretty pleased with himself, but on the way out of the palace he sees Mordecai and gets ticked off all over again. He goes home to his wife, boastful and whining at the same time: "The queen must really like me to invite me to dinner twice, but why (hear that whine in his voice?) won't that miserable Jew Mordecai bow down to me?" His wife and friends advise him to build a gallows and ask the king for permission to hang Mordecai the next day.

Meanwhile, the king has insomnia. With no Sominex on hand, he asks someone to bore him to sleep by reading the royal history book to him. But when the reader gets to the part about Mordecai

"To revolutionize a whole house on the coming of a few visitors betrays not only poor taste, but an absolute lack of character. Let your friends come into your life; let them see you as you are, and not find you trying to be somebody else."

EMMA WHITCOMB BABCOOK

thwarting an assassination attempt, the king's eyes open. Forget about sleep! The man who did this has to be rewarded! At that very moment—we're talking early morning now—Haman strolls in, hoping to catch a breakfast meeting with the king to submit an official request for a hanging. He's looking forward to a big day at the gallows, followed by another intimate dinner with the royal couple. The king sends a servant to find out who's around and finding Haman handy calls him in.

The king asks, "What should I do to honor someone who's done something really great for me?"

Haman is pretty full of himself by this point, what with two dinner invitations in a row and now being called in to see the king. Thinking that he is the one about to be honored as Employee of the Year, Haman lays it on thick, suggesting a new company car, the king's own Hugo Boss suit, and a parade down Fifth Avenue, with commentary by Katie Couric and Matt Lauer on his achievements. Well, okay…at least the Persian equivalent of all that.

Just imagine Haman's utter humiliation—not to mention his seething anger!—when he finds out that the person who will get all this isn't him at all but the despised Mordecai! And even worse, *he's* the one who's going to have to go around telling everyone how great Mordecai is.

After a day of carrying out the king's order with a fake smile pasted on his face, Haman is hardly in the mood for Esther's festivities—particularly after his wife's encouraging words: "Since Mordecai…is of Jewish origin, you cannot stand against him—you will surely come to ruin!" (6:13).

Now the stage is set, and the players are in position. This time, as Esther graciously welcomes the king and Haman to banquet number two, the time is right to speak her request, respectfully but boldly. Even though she knows that now is the time, she doesn't know all of the events that are coming together in this drama being directed by the hand of God. This was one leading lady who knew how to take directions, even when the only part of the script she knew about was her own.

Could Haman's day get any worse? It couldn't have been further from the expectations he had boasted about the night before. Now he finds that the queen hasn't invited him to dinner to honor him, but to condemn him as a traitor who has conspired to kill her. And then, to put a really awful ending to a day that started out horribly, Haman is hanged on the gallows he had built for Mordecai.

"When pride comes, then comes disgrace, but with humility comes wisdom" (Proverbs 11:2). That's pretty much the story of Haman and Esther in a nutshell. Haman's pride caused a more humiliating disgrace than he could have imagined, and Esther's humility put her in a place to act wisely on behalf of her people.

RISE UP!

As I've said, this book is about character, but it's not a how-to manual. There are some things that can't be taught in a book. Sorry, ladies, it's not that easy. Virtues are characteristics that are learned and formed over time. Esther was a woman of virtue. She knew when to hold her tongue and when to speak, when to be bold and when to hold off, when to give and when to ask. Her wisdom came from years of disciplining herself and learning how to listen to God's voice. She had just spent three days humbling herself in fasting and prayer, and she had spent a lifetime learning obedience.

The way we live our life indicates whether we are being formed in virtue or controlled by our sinful nature. Jesus said, "Every good tree bears good fruit, but a bad tree bears bad fruit. A good tree cannot bear bad fruit, and a bad tree cannot bear good fruit" (Matthew 7:17–18). Don't underestimate the power of wisdom, discernment, patience, compassion, kindness, humility, gentleness, love, joy, peace, goodness, faithfulness, self-control, and serving others in Christian hospitality. Be a servant in the Kingdom of God *for such a time as this*.

SEE IT, SAY IT, WALK IT OUT

- "Then Jesus said to his host, 'When you give a luncheon or dinner, do not invite your friends, your brothers or relatives, or your rich neighbors; if you do, they may invite you back and so you will be repaid. But when you give a banquet, invite the poor, the crippled, the lame, the blind, and you will be blessed. Although they cannot repay you, you will be repaid at the resurrection of the righteous.'" (Luke 14:12–14)
- "Share with God's people who are in need. Practice hospitality." (Romans 12:13)
- "Do not forget to entertain strangers, for by so doing some people have entertained angels without knowing it." (Hebrews 13:2)

JUST DO IT!

1. Hospitality starts at home. Liberally perform random acts of kindness (compliments, a word of encouragement, a smile, a thank-you note, a helping hand) to every person in your household this week. After a week has passed, evaluate how these random acts of kindness have affected your relationships and the mood of your home.

    _____
    _____
    _____
    _____
    _____
    _____

_____

_____

2. Encourage a younger girl in her walk with Christ by inviting her over for a "girls' night in." Titus 2:3–5 instructs older women to teach the younger women. If you are nineteen years old, you are an "older woman" to a thirteen-year-old. Is there a younger girl in your church or neighborhood who could benefit from your time and virtuous example?

Take Courage

...forsuchatimeasthis

Then Esther told them to reply to Mordecai:...."I will go in to the king, which is not according to the law; and if I perish, I perish."

ESTHER 4:15–16

And so Queen Esther replied, "If Your Majesty is pleased with me...and wants to grant my request, my petition is that my life and the lives of my people will be spared. For my people and I have been sold to those who would kill, slaughter, and annihilate us."

ESTHER 7:3–4, NLT

TAKE COURAGE

At the mall a few months ago, I saw a teenager wearing a T-shirt that read "Courage—No Fear." It struck me that it should have read "Courage—Fear. Lots of fear!"

You can't write a book about Esther without recognizing what was perhaps her greatest character trait—courage. Esther's courage caused her to put her own life and the lifestyle she'd become accustomed to on the line as she dared to beseech her king and expose Haman's dark plot against the Jews. Because of the courage of one young girl, an entire race was spared. And Esther's courageous actions marked her as a heroine for generations to come.

There is no question that she acted courageously. But was her courage just a natural, spontaneous reaction to her circumstances? I doubt it. You'd better believe it—she was afraid! She *chose* to put her life on the line. Esther was courageous because she acted in the face of fear. Here's my equation for courage:

Courage = Faith > Fear

Courage is not the absence of fear. In fact, there is no courage without fear. Our faith in Christ is simply greater than our fear. It is Christ who gives us our courage, and that courage is faith in action.

One of my favorite passages on courage is found in Joshua 1. The Israelites had just spent forty years wandering in the wilderness, destined for the Promised Land. Moses, who brought them to the threshold of promise, had just died. Joshua, his young aide, was now responsible for leading the nation, and he knew from scouting reports that though this land was their destiny, they would have to fight for it and drive out their enemies one by one. Joshua must have really needed a pep talk, because in this passage God tells him three times to be strong and courageous:

> *"Be strong and courageous,* because you will lead these people to inherit the land I swore to their forefathers to give them. *Be strong and very courageous.* Be careful to obey all the law my servant Moses gave you; do not turn from it to the right or to the left, that you may be successful wherever you go. Do not let this Book of the Law depart from your mouth; meditate on it day and night, so that you may be careful to do everything written in it. Then you will be prosperous and successful. Have I not commanded you? *Be strong and courageous.* Do not be

terrified; do not be discouraged, for the LORD your God will be with you wherever you go." (Joshua 1:6–9, emphasis mine)

Notice that God does not *suggest* courage. He doesn't say, "You might want to think about being courageous." He *commands* it: "Have I not commanded you? Be strong and courageous." That also means that courage is not a feeling. Courage is a choice.

Many times in Scripture we are told to "take courage." What does it mean to *take* courage? If it is something we are supposed to *take,* we can't expect to automatically possess it. If you're waiting until you *feel* courageous, you'll never take that first bold baby step of courage. We must take hold of our heavenly Father's hand and step out like a child in courage.

COURAGE TO DIE

On April 20, 1999, at Columbine High School, two young women exhibited the ultimate expression of courage. Cassie Bernal and Rachel Scott, two young modern-day Esthers, had the courage to die for Christ. They courageously held on to their faith in Christ in the face of death. These were their final moments of courage:

Read about Cassie and Rachel and other courageous stories in **Columbine Courage** *by Ron Luce.*

A student near Cassie in the library that day recalled that the killers noticed her because she was praying. They walked over to her and asked her if she believed in God. Cassie paused for a moment and said, "Yes." Immediately she was shot in the head at nearly point-blank range.[9]

Rachel was sitting outside the library with her friend Richard Castaldo. Without warning, fellow students Eric Harris and Dylan Klebold opened fire, severing Richard's spine and shooting Rachel twice in her legs and once in her torso. As Richard lay stunned and Rachel attempted to crawl to safety, the shooters began to walk away, only to return seconds later. At that point Harris reportedly grabbed Rachel by her hair, held her head up, and asked her the question:

"Do you believe in God?"

"You know I do," replied Rachel.

"Then go be with Him," replied Harris before shooting her in the head.[10]

These two young women faced their moment of crisis with the same "If I die, I die" courage that Esther did. Their boldness forces us all to ask ourselves, *What would I have done?*

> *"You gain strength, courage and confidence by every experience in which you really stop to look fear in the face.... You must do the thing which you think you cannot do."*
>
> ELEANOR ROOSEVELT

COURAGE TO LIVE

Cassie and Rachel displayed courage the day of the shootings at Columbine, but their courage to die isn't what makes these modern-day Esthers so incredible; it was their courage to live that should challenge us.

Cassie Bernal was an unlikely martyr. Like other martyrs throughout history, she didn't have a death wish. But she did have a troubled past, one that included witchcraft, drugs, and rebellion. She had even threatened to kill her own parents at one point. Through the influence of a friend who was deep in the occult and the shock rock music of groups like Marilyn Manson, Cassie became caught up in a world of darkness.

A radical encounter with God two years before her death rescued Cassie from her downward spiral. But what allowed her to die heroically were the deaths she died daily as she made choices to overcome her past. No matter what the cost—loss of reputation, harassment from her old friends—Cassie courageously chose every day to die to herself and live for Christ.

Two days before she died, Cassie wrote this poem:

Now I have given up everything else.

I have found it to be the only way to really know Christ

and to experience the mighty power that

brought Him back to life again

and to find out what that means to suffer and to die with Him.

So, whatever it takes, I will be one who lives in the fresh newness of

life of those who are alive from the dead.

In *She Said Yes,* Cassie's mother, Misty Bernal, wrote:

The world looks at Cassie's "yes" of April 20, but we need to look at the daily "yes" she said day after day, month after month, before giving that final answer. I know that her death was not a waste, but a triumph of honesty and courage. To me, Cassie's life says that it is better to die for what you believe, than to live a lie. [11]

Rachel Scott was an average teenager—except for her not-so-average walk with the Lord. She was an all-American girl: smart, pretty, and well liked. What set her apart, though, was her intense and intimate walk with God. She was a modern-day Esther in many ways.

The authors of *Rachel's Tears* describe Rachel again and again as real. Her life and her faith were authentic. She broke away from the popular pack to reach out with kindness and compassion to kids who had fallen through the cracks: "Rachel's misfits." She loved drama and on several occasions used it to give bold expression of her faith. Her youth group, Breakaway, was her life. Her sister remembers watching her at one of their gatherings:

> *Courage has nothing to do with your determination to be great. It has to do with what you decide in that moment when you are called upon. No matter how small the moment, or how personal, it is a moment when your life takes a turn and the lives of those around you take a turn because of you.*
> RITA DOVE,
> FIRST AFRICAN-AMERICAN
> U.S. POET LAUREATE

I got to see her sing her lungs out and praise God with all her heart. I got to see her dance before the Lord and worship Him any way she wanted to. I got to see her fight her battles on her knees in prayer and really cry out to God…. I got to see where she got her strength, her joy, her dreams, her inspiration, her wisdom, her boldness, her humility, her honesty, her passion to see lives touched by God, her anointing, her gifts, her talents, her gentleness, her creativity, her discernment, her acceptance of others, her ability to see the "brighter" side, her ability to see the "bigger picture," her compassion, her understanding, her quest for knowledge, her quest for truth, her open mind, her open heart, her selflessness, her peace of mind, her awesome sense of humor, her freedom from sin, her faith like a child, her hope, her love for people, and her love for God! I got to see God mold my sister into something beautiful because her heart was willing to allow Him to do so. That beauty radiated outwardly, but more importantly, it came from within, and she didn't even know it. She was real. [12]

But deciding to "walk her talk" also brought ridicule, mockery, and rejection by friends. She took heat for her beliefs, but she was willing to pay the price. She was willing to lay down her life every day. In her journal she wrote:

I am not going to apologize for speaking the name of Jesus,
I am not going to justify my faith to them, and
I am not going to hide the light that God has put into me.
If I have to sacrifice everything...I will. [13]

Cassie and Rachel's courage has encouraged the resolve of a generation to live boldly for God as Darlene, a youth minister, notes:

> What the devil means for evil, God can use for good. The devil thought he was getting rid of some Christian teenagers, but what he did caused hundreds of teenagers to stand up for their faith instead of being wishy-washy. The shootings made them realize that they are in warfare, and there is nothing that can separate them from the love of God. [14]

DARE TO LIVE COURAGEOUSLY

The chances are slim that you will experience something like Cassie and Rachel did that day at Columbine, but that doesn't mean that God isn't calling you to courage. He may call you, as He did Cassie, to resist peer pressure or to fight Satan's dark influence with the light of Christ. Or God may require you, as He did Rachel, to step out of your comfort zone to reach out to someone on the fringe, extending friendship and acceptance. Or He may put you in a position to boldly speak your moral convictions and faith to the crowd, amid heckles, snickering, or rejection.

It takes courage to do these things—to be set apart, to walk in purity, to obey, to be authentic, to make godly choices even if no one else does, to speak out against injustice, and to offer kindness, gentleness, and love to those who persecute you. But that's what Jesus did, and we are His disciples.

Let the words of this song encourage your faith to be great.

Point of Grace—"Any Road, Any Cost"

FROM LIFE, LOVE, AND OTHER MYSTERIES
Written by Scott Krippayne and Tony Wood
© 1996 BMG Songs, Inc. (ASCAP) All rights reserved. Used by permission.

Leaving the safe and familiar,
with their heads set on a heavenly prize,
there were some who laid down their nets,
and some who laid down their lives
Not sure where they are going,
but they did not have to know,
'cause they knew who had called them,
and they said, "We will go."
Down any road at any cost,
Wherever You lead we will follow,
because we know
that You've called us to take up our cross

down any road at any cost.
It may be fear that we're feeling
when we see what we must sacrifice,
but You promised You'll go with us,
so we'll trust with our lives
down any road, at any cost.

Without courage, you will never grow in character. Courage grows little by little, with every act of obedience and through every trial and temptation. Have the courage to walk boldly in character every day and to do the right thing even when no one sees you or when it's inconvenient, no matter what the cost.

AN *E*STHER MOMENT

From the journal of a modern-day Esther:

Smile my love
and laugh in the devil's face,
for the Lord has made your strength
perfect,
your rest complete
and your path straight.
All for His glory
and your eternal happiness.

—Lisa Dauffenbach[15]

Rise Up!

Esther showed amazing courage when she boldly stated, "If I perish, I perish." Once her destiny was revealed through crisis and she began to realize that perhaps she had come to her position *for such a time as this,* the courage of her conviction rose up. She chose at that moment to become an advocate, to face her fear, and to trust God for the outcome. From that moment, she took courage and began to move decisively and with bold resolve.

God is looking for our willingness to go down any road He leads us at any cost. He will supply the courage in the face of fear when we need it. "He will never leave you nor forsake you" (Deuteronomy 31:6). You can always take courage in that. When you cling to Him for your strength, you, too, will have the courage of Esther to walk in your destiny, *for such a time as this.*

See It, Say It, Walk It Out

- "So be strong and take courage, all you who put your hope in the LORD!" (Psalm 31:24, NLT)
- "Yet our God gave us the courage to declare his Good News to you boldly, even though we were surrounded by many who opposed us." (1 Thessalonians 2:2, NLT)
- "And now, dear children, continue to live in fellowship with Christ so that when he returns, you will be full of courage and not shrink back from him in shame." (1 John 2:28, NLT)

Just Do It!

1. Pray

   God, help me to walk in courage for You this week. Convict me. Reveal to me areas of my life where I am not walking in courage, for fear is not of God. Give me an opportunity to be Christlike in courage this week. Help me to recognize this divine appointment when it comes.

Give me eyes to see and ears to hear. Speak to me Your will in that situation and empower me by Your Holy Spirit to succeed, bringing glory and honor to You. Amen.

2. Take Courage
    Just look at the lives of some of the modern-day Esthers we've talked about:
    - Tori's courage at an early age to stand alone and position herself before God even if she looked different from the crowd;
    - Sara and Dana's courage to live lives of purity;
    - Dana Elizabeth and Kristina's courage to be set apart for preparation and God's purpose;
    - Nicole's courage to respond to the crisis of diabetes and use her disease to help others;
    - Jenni's courage to get real, risk receiving God's unconditional love, and be set apart for godly restoration and divine destiny;
    - Erin's courage to choose to listen to the Lord's leading, which took her out of the game, so to speak, but put her back in the game with God;
    - Marian's courage and boldness to proclaim her faith in the midst of opposition;
    - Our Asian-American Esther's courage and faith to fast and pray;
    - Rachel and Cassie's courage to live for and confess Christ.

3. 📓 Journal It:
    God gives divine appointments with courage daily if you are willing to listen for His call. What divine appointment did you have with courage this week?

    _____

    _____

_____
_____
_____

How did you respond?

_____
_____
_____
_____

4. Write your own confession of courage.
   "When courage is required, I will…

_____
_____
_____
_____

Generation Esther—Rise Up!

...forsuchatimeasthis

*"Rise up; this matter is in your hands.
We will support you, so take courage and do it."*

EZRA 10:4

As cohost of *The 700 Club*, I am privileged to see and hear up-to-date information about what is happening in the Christian church throughout the world, and I have noticed a recent trend. I've seen the Holy Spirit igniting this theme of the mantle and message of Esther in many settings: youth conferences, revivals, grass-roots movements, and schools. Even the Veggie Tales video *Esther* speaks to the youngest of this generation, the little Esthers to come.

Pop culture has labeled you everything from Generation D (digital) to Generation X, Y, and Z. From my perspective, the observers and definers of pop culture have missed the growing movement of Generation E. Generation Esther is quietly but courageously rising up. Will you be found in her ranks?

It's my prayer that this book has begun to give you a vision of destiny and revealed some of the disciplines and character that will position you to become a modern-day Esther. I pray that you will recognize your position as a princess in God's court, embrace the blessings and responsibilities of royalty, and join ranks with other young women of destiny. Now is the time to link arms in solidarity with other modern-day Esthers who have made the same radical choice you have. God has brought you to this place and time in His-story and prepared you to be set apart *for such a time as this.*

JUST DO IT!

You know how on your computer you can use a previous document as a template to create a new document or file with new information? Well, in your mental computer, do this exercise:

> Pretend you have a document that contains the Esther story entitled "Esther." Now place your arrow on "file" and drag down to "save as." Sound too much like computer class? Well hold on, 'cause here's the best part. Retitle that document by replacing "Esther" with your name. Now, using Esther's story as a template, adjust it according to your experiences and particular circumstances. Use this book and the lessons of character we've seen in it to help write your own Esther story.

RiseUp

Generation *E*—E-Mail Me!

God is moving among many young women today, women who are making the bold decision to become the generation that rises up for God. I hope and pray that this book touches your heart and impacts your life in such a way that you—and your friends—make that decision, too!

Please drop by my Web site at www.lisaryan.tv and tell me how God is working in your life. While you're there you can read updates from me, comments from other readers, and a weekly Generation E devotional.

Are you a modern-day Esther? Or do you know someone who is? Send me the story at lisaryan@christianity.com. Until then, may the Lord Jesus Christ, the God of Esther, place His hand upon your life, renewing the old, affirming the present, and giving purpose and passion to your destiny in the kingdom of God, for such a time as this.

Your friend,

Lisa

www.generationesther.com

lisa@generationesther.com

1. Darlene Sala, *Created for a Purpose* (Uhrichsville, Ohio: Barbour and Co., Inc., 2000), 75.
2. Ibid., 76.
3. Michelle McKinney, *The Power of Femininity* (Eugene, Ore.: Harvest House, 1999), 43.
4. © 2001 by Lisa Dauffenbach. From the journal of a modern-day Esther: Lisa Dauffenbach.
5. © 2001 by Lisa Dauffenbach. From the journal of a modern-day Esther: Lisa Dauffenbach.
6. Margery Williams Bianco, *The Velveteen Rabbit* (New York: Doubleday, 1958).
7. © 2001 by Lisa Dauffenbach. From the journal of a modern-day Esther: Lisa Dauffenbach.
8. © 2001 by Lisa Dauffenbach. From the journal of a modern-day Esther: Lisa Dauffenbach.
9. Misty Bernal, *She Said Yes* (Farmington, Pa.: Plough Pub House, 1999), 13.
10. Darrell Scott, et al., *Rachel's Tears* (Nashville, Tenn.: Thomas Nelson, 2000), 92.
11. Bernal, *She Said Yes.*
12. Scott, *Rachel's Tears,* 118–9.
13. Ibid., 97.
14. Ron Luce, *Columbine Courage* (Nashville, Tenn.: J. Countryman, 2000), 57.
15. © 2001 by Lisa Dauffenbach. From the journal of a modern-day Esther: Lisa Dauffenbach.

YOUR PERSONAL STUDY GUIDE TO FINDING IDENTITY, PURPOSE, AND A PASSION

For Such a Time as This Study Guide

Just as the biblical Esther needed a year of preparations before she became queen, a modern Esther needs preparation to fulfill her destiny. In this in-depth companion study to *For Such a Time as This,* young women follow Esther's example to shape their unique gifts and destinies in a way that will set them apart from the world. Interactive lessons equip them to develop character traits such as courage, purity, obedience, and humility—transforming them into mature women of God.

ISBN 1-59052-174-9

YOU'RE MORE THAN JUST A PRETTY FACE.

Just as Esther was set apart for her destiny by her character and her commitment to God, He is preparing young women today to influence their generation for Him. This companion book to *For Such a Time as This* profiles the lives of several modern-day Esthers, from headliners like Rebecca St. James, Heather Mercer, and Dayna Curry to unexpected heroines. Each girl's story illustrates important character strengths, such as purity, friendship, honesty, advocacy, prayer, servanthood, and courage, that influenced her response to challenging choices and cultural pressures. These profiles will inspire every young woman who wonders what God can do through her.

ISBN 1-59052-194-3